WANTED:
A GOOD PASTOR

**The Characteristics, Skills, and Attitudes
Every Effective Church Leader Needs**

JONAS ARRAIS

DEDICATION

To My Family:
First of all, to my wife and lover,
Raquel, my partner in ministry
for nearly thirty years. Also to my
sons, Tiago and Andre, who are
preparing to be good pastors, and
to their wives, Paula and Natalia,
who are great gifts from heaven.

ACKNOWLEDGMENTS

To the General Conference Ministerial
Association for their support.
To Judith A. Thomas for developmental
funding. And Ricardo Bacchus for outstanding
assistance in the preparation of this book.

CONTENTS

FOREWORD

In these last days, one of our most pressing needs is pastoral leadership. To truly fulfill the gospel commission, our leaders must possess an intimate understanding of their critical role. They must answer their call with fervor and passion. We need pastors who understand their role in unleashing their members, "the priesthood of all believers", for their ministry to the people of this world.

This book addresses vital components of effective pastoring. The core attitudes, training, and skills needed to enable and equip God's people are presented in a way that motivates and trains leaders to apply them practically.

The foundational truth that a deep, personal connection to God and an understanding of the power of prayer are central to a pastor's ministry and personal life is highlighted. The pastor's family life, integrity, people skills, and leadership are also brought into focus. The vital ministry of visitation, an essential component of pastoral work, is especially emphasized.

What a privilege it is to be allowed by our Lord to serve His people! The rewards of effective and spiritually empowered ministry are amazing. This book will help pastors and church leaders avoid burnout from ineffective and misguided ministry efforts. When we join our Lord in His work and do it in accordance with the principles He has given us, the results will shine for eternity!

Jerry N. Page
General Conference Ministerial Secretary

INTRODUCTION

" *Then I will give you shepherds after my own heart, who will lead you with knowledge and understanding.*"
—JEREMIAH 3:15

We need good pastors. Today! In many congregations, members are desperately crying *Lord, send us a good pastor.* Church administrators are seeking out leaders as well, knowing that it is God's desire for His church.

Are you a good, effective pastor? Does your spouse see you as a good pastor? Do your church members think of you as a good pastor?

What does it mean to be a good, successful pastor? Is a good pastor one who can take a congregation of 50 and increase it to 500 in just a couple of years? Is a good pastor one who has a heart for mission and can raise thousands of dollars to support missionary activities around the world?

A pastor friend of mine once said, "If you want to be a good pastor, you should teach your church members three things: how to pray, how to study the Bible, and how to share their faith." A former church leader in the South American Division used to say that what separates the average from the extraordinary is the details. He illustrated this by saying, "Why is a Mercedes so expensive and a Lada (a Russian car) so cheap? Both of them have doors, an engine, seats, and wheels. Ah! The details make the difference!"

When I envision a good pastor, many pictures come to mind. I see someone who is balanced—blessed with a combination of characteristics, skills, and attitudes. I see someone who knows what he needs to know, what he has to do, and who he must be. I wrote this book with a strong conviction that there are many ideas to share and things to learn about pastoring. I am, by no means, a perfect pastor. It is my desire to do more and be better in my life as a pastor. In almost thirty years of ministry, I've travelled to many

INTRODUCTION

places around the world and attended countless pastoral advisories and meetings. I have had many opportunities to talk to other pastors, their spouses, and church members. I have found that the majority of pastors are committed, versatile, and do far more than they were called, or even trained, to do. On the other hand, I have also seen pastors who are struggling. Their church members complain of poor preaching, non-existent visitations, and a lack of leadership. Very often, this leads to relationships with their congregations that are far from ideal.

Through this book, I hope to assist my colleagues in ministry and improve their sacred work by presenting some pastoral skills and responsibilities essential for ministerial competency. However, this book isn't restricted to pastors. It is also for elders and other church leaders who dedicate themselves to serving their congregation. It is my desire to support these local church elders and others by providing an overview of what it means to be a true pastor in their church.

The rewards of being a good pastor are numerous. I truly believe there is no other calling more noble or joyous than being called by God to minister to His people. It is my prayer that you are deeply enriched and blessed as you read, discover, and live out what it means to be a good pastor.

Jonas Arrais

Chapter 1

THE ESSENCE OF A PASTOR

Authentic ministry comes from within. It is not the result of a hierarchal position, or the completion of a Masters or Doctoral degree. Ministry reflects the essence of a pastor's life. Above all else, authentic ministry is God living through you. It is more than what you do; it is who you are. It is your God-given essence.

As a pastor, your first calling should be to nurture your own heart and your own spiritual vitality. It must be the foundation of both your life and ministry. It is through this that you will discover your identity and ability in the God who uses the foolish, broken, and needy to accomplish His will.

A pastor's life is often dominated by various obligations. Tending to the minutia of administrative responsibilities can leave little time to apply your gifts and pursue your passion for ministry. As a result, it's easy to feel unfulfilled or disconnected from your calling.

No doubt, there are many other important leadership qualities. But remember, all genuine leadership begins with desperation—the acceptance that we are all helpless sinners in great need of a Savior. Desperation moves us to surrender. We seek God in His Word. We cry out to Him in prayer. We learn to trust. We believe in His great and precious promises. And we are free, living a life of love and service, glorifying our heavenly Father.

Your relationship with God is the foundation, the core, the energy that propels your life of service. If you could dedicate even just an hour from your busy schedule to visit with God, the benefits would manifest in all aspects of your life. This quiet communion can be a refuge—a rare moment when you're allowed to forget sermons and committees and renew your spirituality. It's a safe place to stop and reconnect with your calling and your Creator, and to pray *Lord, here I am; what do You have to say to me today?* This daily recommitment is essential to not only your spiritual well being, but to your ministry as a whole. Effective ministry only grows out of an intimate experience with God.[1]

An important part of your pastoral duties is to guide and grow your congregation along their spiritual walk. Yet despite all the nurturing you do for others, you can find yourself struggling to care for your own physical and spiritual needs. In the book *Hard to Be Holy,* Paul and Libby Whethan suggest that a poor relationship with God can lead to high levels of burnout in pastors. This means that those who do not feel particularly close to God in their own lives are especially vulnerable to ministerial problems.[2]

Spiritual authenticity is a requisite trait of all pastors. Regardless of all other societal expectations, you must strive to draw closer to God. True, it is possible to meet the expectations of God and men. But if ever you were forced to choose, always choose God. Hate sin and love righteousness in all aspects of your life.[3]

AVOID HYPOCRISY IN MINISTRY

As pastors, we possess knowledge and understanding of the scriptures the average person does not. We've attended schools and seminaries, spent years studying the Word of God. Yet hypocrisy runs rampant throughout our profession. Why is that? We, of all people, should know better.

In his article on hypocrisy, Kevin Haag says, "The word hypocrisy originates from the Greek language as a theatrical term. One actor often played multiple roles in the same play by disguising himself with a series of masks. The actor was called a 'hypocrite' because he had two or more faces. The idea of a person being 'two-faced' evolved, describing someone who said one thing and did another.

A hypocrite lives a lie; he tries to make the outside appear better than the inside. When the deception of a hypocrite is exposed, many people are hurt, disappointed, and disheartened. A hyp-

> " *It is easier to cope with a bad conscience than with a bad reputation.*"
> –FRIEDRICH NIETZSCHE

ocrite causes the loss of his own trustworthiness and the integrity of others."[4]

In the Sermon on the Mount (Matthew 5-7), Jesus commands us not to be hypocritical in our giving (Matthew 6:1-4), our prayers (Matthew 6:5-15), and in our fasting (Matthew 6:16-18). This is applicable to our lives and ministry today. On almost every occasion that Jesus rebuked hypocrisy, His words were directed to the Pharisees and scribes. They appeared honest, devout disciples. But within, they were full of corruption.

In Matthew 23:3, Jesus says, "But do not do what they do, for they do not practice what they preach." This begs the troubling question *Do all pastors practice what they preach?* Pastors are often singled out as being hypocritical. They live with the burden of higher societal expectations. And even the Bible warns that they "will be judged more strictly" (James 3:1). This standard can seem unrealistically high.

Of course, no pastor can consistently practice what he preaches. If we could only preach on subjects we have mastered, there would be very little on which to preach. The good news is that we have been called to preach the truth from the Word of God. When we deliver a sermon, we proclaim God's Word not only to the congregation, but to ourselves as well.

Ultimately, hypocrisy is more about fooling yourself than fooling others.

PURSUE INTEGRITY

The adage *the life of a minister is the life of his ministry* is as true now as ever. Every day we make choices about what to do and how to live. Our lives must reflect the code of inviolable absolutes that govern our actions. We are defined by our behavior. Paul captures the importance of personal integrity in Acts 24:16: "So I strive always to keep my conscience clear before God and man." At the heart of integrity is a determination to live in the presence of God with a clear conscience.

Integrity is a crucial component of authentic ministry. The importance of living a life of

> **"** *Integrity has no need of rules."*
>
> –ALBERT CAMUS

15

integrity cannot be overstated. For those who serve as pastors and proclaim the truth, the onus to live the truth that we proclaim is always upon us.[5] Are you the same person during the week and on Sabbath morning? When we pretend, we are being the double-minded man of James 1:8–"Such a person is double-minded and unstable in all they do." Duplicity, however, is counter to our God-given inner ethic and damages our health emotionally and spiritually. A wholesome and integrated life with harmony between actions and beliefs, honors the One in whose image we are made.

Eric Liddell, a missionary to China, gives insight into the meaning of integrity and suggests four simple tests to evaluate our personal integrity:[6]

1. *Am I truthful?*
2. *Am I honest?*
3. *Am I pure?*
4. *Am I selfish?*

When we surrender ourselves to God and allow Him to change us from within, we take on His character. This change is evident both inside and out. We begin to function as God intended, marrying righteous motives with righteous acts. And in turn, we discover a sense of fulfillment, peace and joy that comes from a life of integrity.

Hypocrisy is the ultimate frustration. Its solution is confession and repentance—so simple, yet so difficult. And we often find ourselves going to enormous lengths just to avoid it. Don't let hypocrisy hinder your ability to be an effective instrument of God.

MAINTAIN INTEGRITY

Without integrity, all our efforts are in vain. Nothing erodes a pastor's credibility more than dishonesty and moral ambiguity. We cannot allow it to seep into our churches and communities. But how do we protect ourselves? Here are some suggestions:

If in doubt, don't! Doubt can leave you feeling "blown and tossed by the wind" (James 1:6). These feelings of uncertainty can ripple out and affect those you lead spiritually. Give yourself more time before making big changes in your church and don't move too quickly. Pray. Seek godly counsel from those who strive to have the mind of Christ.

Avoid all appearance of misconduct. Do not allow yourself to get into precarious situations where your intentions could be questioned. For example, when a minister puts himself in a situation where he is alone with someone of the opposite sex, he is playing with fire. When it comes to dealing with church money, be cautious and use proper accounting practices. Be able to back up your decisions with an unquestionable assurance, in your heart, that you have done God's will (1 Thessalonians 5:22, 23).[7]

Never consider yourself above temptation. People say *It couldn't happen to me.* But we must be aware of our intrinsic vulnerability. Our first defense should be an attitude of humility that says *I'm human and my heart is deceitful.* We should have a holy fear of assuming we are never beyond temptation.[8]

Maintain self-awareness. Recommit yourself to God on a daily basis. Proverbs 4:23 says, "Above all else, guard your heart, for everything you do flows from it." Maintaining that daily walk with the Lord is absolutely imperative. I find that, in temptation of any kind, I need to continually remind myself of God's omniscience and omnipresence. God sees everything in my life. He is always with me. It is the devil that says *No one will ever know.* This is true of any kind of temptation. If I am convinced that God is always with me and He sees everything, then I can act accordingly. "I discipline my body like an athlete, training it to do what it should. Otherwise, I fear that after preaching to others I myself might be disqualified" (1 Corinthians 9:27, NLT).[9] This verse underscores the importance of integrity and cultivating your relationship with God. Spirituality, like your body, requires constant care and maintenance.

> " *Character is higher than intellect.*"
> –Ralph Waldo Emerson

Guard your mind. The Bible is unequivocal on this point. The battle for sin always begins in the mind. If you lose the battle in your mind, you've lost the war. "Each person is tempted when they are dragged away by their own evil desire and enticed. Then, after desire has conceived, it gives birth to sin; and sin, when it is full-grown, gives birth to death" (James 1:14-15).

Spend time with the Lord every day. Your ministry takes the shape of your personal walk with God. A pastor who reads the Bible daily, meditates upon the Word, delights in it, and makes his decisions in light of God's Word, will not listen to wrong counsel or make personal decisions he will later regret (Psalms 1:1-2). Daily Bible study is crucial to maintaining a level of intimacy with God.[10]

BE HONEST WITH YOURSELF

Society holds pastors to a high standard. We are supposed to be great leaders, exemplary in our faith. Yet we are only human. How are we to live up to these expectations? More importantly, what does God require of us? Are we to be perfect? Are we somehow lacking in our ministry? Looking back through the years, sins, faults, and failures litter my life. But I also see the kind and loving hand of a merciful Savior. And despite it all, I can declare, with great happiness *God has been good to me! He has shown me much mercy and grace, far more than I deserve.*

When I look back at my nearly thirty years in the ministry, I see truth and an earnest desire to minister. But I also see times when pride and ego played a role! My work, methods, and dreams were at times mixed with my own ideas or plans as I sought to find the will of God in my life. Although successful at times, I recall times when I acted on my own strengths and strategies instead of God's.

I know that there are others who wrestle with similar situations. In drawing from my own experience, I hope I can help others recognize their weaknesses and motivate them to turn to Jesus for guidance.

> " *Your life may be the only Bible some people read."*
> –AUTHOR UNKNOWN

As ministers of the gospel, are we always honest with God? He has given us an awesome task to perform. But, by using our own strength, intelligence, and experiences, we can still fail. We may succeed in our own eyes, and even man's eyes, but filtered through the eyes of God and His Word, we may be an utter failure and not know it!

Many times pastors equate success with accomplishments. God is the only one who knows what we are really accomplishing, and why. It would be sad to come to the end of our ministry only to discover that God has rejected much of our efforts. This may be shocking to some, but God is more concerned about *why* we did something, than the what and the how. "When we stand before God to account for what we have done, all ministry without Him is going to be sounding brass and tinkling cymbals. It may have looked good statistically in this life, but how will it really look for eternity?"[11]

What drives us? Is it recognition, money, duty, obligation, prestige, ego? Are any of these justifiable motivations for ministry?

Being is more important than doing. Ministry will never take the place of devotion to God. Often, our motivation can be clouded by a desire to work hard, to build a bigger church, to baptize more people, and to protect the church from heresies and false doctrine. In the process, it's easy to lose the focus of Jesus' primary interest—loving Him!

GOD'S REMEDY

When the Lord began to show me what I was doing and where my priorities were, I could see more clearly His expectations of me.

I pray differently now. I pray for His love and guidance in all I do. My prayer goes something like this: *Heavenly Father, I come to you in the name of Jesus. You know what is already on my heart and mind. I know that there is absolutely nothing I can hide from you. There are many things in my life that I don't know how to handle. I need your Spirit, strength, love, boldness, courage, compassion, guidance, and a renewing of the Spirit as I seek to do your will. Keep my love fresh and where I have failed, let me return to 'my first love!' I repent, as I have been caught up in doing so much of the work of the church, and have let my relationship with you slip. Restore me and fill me again with your precious Holy Spirit. AMEN!*

I thank God there is a remedy for my problems and struggles! I can repent. Jesus says that I can begin anew. My only motivation to do God's work must be my love for Him and my desire to please Him.

CAN YOU BE A GOOD PASTOR WITHOUT FULLY SURRENDERING TO GOD AND ALLOWING HIM TO GUIDE YOUR LIFE?

Questions for reflection, consideration, or discussion:

1. What does the expression *authentic ministry comes from within* mean to you?
2. Why is hypocrisy a big problem in pastoral ministry?
3. How can hypocrisy damage your spiritual life and ministry?
4. Why is integrity so important for an effective pastoral ministry?
5. In your opinion, what is the secret to developing a ministry of which God approves?

Chapter 2

AN EFFECTIVE PREACHER

There was a grocer who had never heard his local minister preach. Yet he always insisted the minister was a good preacher. When asked why, he replied, "I know he is a good preacher because the members of his parish have started paying their bills."

It is almost impossible to picture a good pastor without good preaching skills. Most often, good pastors are well known and respected for their outstanding preaching. Hundreds of books have been written on the subject of preaching. With such an abundance of material to choose from, every preacher would do well to explore this subject. For our purposes, however, let us focus on what it means to *be* a good preacher, as opposed to discussing methods or strategies.

DEFINITION OF A GOOD PREACHER

Richard J. Krejcir, a church growth specialist, notes, "The number one reason for church growth is the preaching ability of the pastor."[1] So what defines a good preacher? Is it style, content, delivery, human interest, enlightening illustrations, humor? All of the above? None of the above? Or is it the capacity to preach a great sermon in a short amount of time? Or the ability to motivate people to hunger for the Word of God?

Let us focus on God's expectations of a good preacher. Paul wrote to Timothy, "If you point these things out to the brothers and sisters, you will be a good minister of Christ Jesus, nourished on the truths of the faith and of the good teaching that you have followed" (1 Timothy 4:6). A good preacher reminds people of what God's Word says. It is not the job of a preacher to convince or persuade. It is simply to relay God's message to His people.

While some preachers command more attention and respect than others, anyone preaching the true Word of God should be held in high esteem. God values all who do His work. For this reason, a good preacher never uses sermon time only to entertain people, but to preach the message.[2]

Most people recognize a good sermon when they hear one. Yet, they may have difficulty articulating what exactly makes it a good sermon. For those of us who try to preach *good sermons,* it is useful to understand what elicits these positive responses from our listeners.

Of course, every listener looks for different things in a preacher. A listener's personal religious philosophy will determine their perception of the sermon. Those with an intellectual appreciation of scripture might expect something different than one with a more practical approach of the work of the Holy Spirit. Learning style also determines the effectiveness of a sermon. Some listeners learn best through reflection; others prefer a more active and participatory approach. Culture also plays a significant role. Our roots, generation, denomination, economic situation, and gender all play a part in determining our response to a sermon and the preacher. Still, preaching is preaching. There are certain unilateral truths. If the following things are in place, we can be confident that our sermons will be well appreciated and lead to the kinds of responses we expect. These are the factors that will result in *good* and maybe even *great* preaching.

A good sermon is rooted in the Bible. A sermon ought to find its footing in the Word of God. A preacher can say many fine things, but if the listener doesn't feel the sermon has led them to a deeper understanding of the Bible, it falls short. This means that the Bible must be used as more than window dressing or a jumping-off point. Scripture is the foundation of every good sermon. Good preachers understand that God still speaks through His Word. When it comes to good preaching, the Bible is where the power is.

A good sermon helps people hear God. This is as helpful a definition of preaching as I know. Preachers connect people with the voice of God. If a listener does not sense that they are in the presence of God and are hearing something meaningful from Him, then the sermon is not effective. As such, good sermons do not have to conform to any particular structure. The sermon, as a medium, is flexible. It responds to the interests and concerns of any culture and situation. If it helps people hear what God is saying, it is a good sermon, regardless of style. This underlines a dependence on the Scriptures.

A good sermon is easily understood. Some preachers confuse complexity with depth. In my experience, simple truths are the most profound. Listeners understand good preaching. Good preachers work to understand the language, the culture, and the interests of those to whom they preach. They work hard to clarify and unify their presentation so there is no confusion about their message. In most cases, good sermons offer one idea—an idea presented simply to encourage appreciation and application.

A good sermon exalts Jesus Christ. As Christian preachers, every sermon we preach should exalt Jesus Christ. While not every text is directly Christological, I believe that every sermon ought to be.

These four principles apply to every good sermon I have ever heard. A good sermon integrates the person and presence of God with the person and presence of the preacher. The divine and the human collaborate in the mystery that is good preaching.

This definition can be applied to any preacher in any other religion or ideology. Notice that the definition of a good preacher doesn't include strength of one's own faith.

First, a good preacher must have a *compelling vision*. He must be able to verbalize and communicate a crystal clear vision that the listener can visualize. For example, he must be able to skillfully describe a fictional place in such minute detail that you begin to believe the place is real! Secondly, a good preacher *communicates forcefully*. It's not enough to communicate clearly. He must do so in a manner that commands attention. He must be entertaining. His words must be gripping. He must be charismatic. He must not be ignored.

Finally, a good preacher must relate to the listener on a personal level. It is not enough that a preacher paint a beautiful picture of the ultimate goal. To the one person in the congregation who says *I am flawed and cannot attain the spirituality that others have,* a good preacher has the ability to address that one person's specific shortcomings and reach out to him personally.

Either quit preaching or take the time to do it right. Like most things in life, preaching is a skill that can be taught and with practice you can actually become good at it.

Unfortunately, good preachers are in short supply—not just those who teach from the pulpit, but those who truly understand the meaning of ministry and can deliver a powerful sermon. Many churches express discontent with their pastor's preaching.

In a survey of pastors that covered areas of ministry such as administration, teaching, preaching, pastoring, and church business, two questions were asked. The first was *what do you think is the most important area of ministry?* Overwhelmingly, the response was *preaching.*[3]

The second question was *what occupies most of your time?"* Their answer was just as decisive—*administration.* Preaching was last on the list. How tragic! That which we feel is most important is what we do the least.

PREACHERS MUST PREACH

Preaching is the primary responsibility of a pastor. A good pastor spends much time in prayer before he even opens the Word of God. His top priority is to nurture his congregation through God's Word.

A church member once approached me with mixed feelings about her pastor. On the one hand, she appreciated his dedication to visitation. Yet, his preaching left much to be desired. Visitation is an essential aspect of ministry. But alone, it is not enough.

Almost a year later, she came to me again. I could tell she was frustrated. "I am concerned about my pastor," she said. "Not only is he a weak preacher, but he is also always inviting guest speakers to replace him on the pulpit. I am very disappointed in him."

Pastors must be preachers. They cannot flee or avoid the pulpit. While good preachers are always present in congregations and are delighted to preach, guest speakers should be an exception. A pastor is not supposed to sit idly and watch his members do his job.

Some preachers become sidetracked and diverted from their intended message. They are carried about with every wind of popular opinion. They substitute preaching for drama and entertainment. They hold festivals, seminars, and dream up gimmicks instead of preaching the Word of God.

Compare today's pastor with the prophets of old. Take Jonah, for example. God uses three words that characterize not only his ministry, but also the ministry of all ministers: "Arise, go . . . and proclaim" (Jonah 1:2, AMP). The preacher must not flee the pulpit. His ministry must be inspired by these three verbs—arise, go, and proclaim!

THERE IS NO EXCUSE

Church members don't like seeing a pastor avoid the pulpit or preach a weak sermon. They may never talk to him about it, but they will certainly be disappointed. Pastors are full-time church workers. Finding time for sermon preparation is part of the job description. There is no excuse for a pastor to avoid the pulpit or deliver a poor message.

Good preaching is incredibly important and must be relevant to the church. It does not matter how big your church is, how many times you have to preach during a month, or how many congregations you pastor. Let nothing take the place of preaching. Let no concert, movie, or drama presentation be given as a substitute for the preaching of the Gospel.

Preachers must preach because preaching is the power of God unto salvation. Preaching is doctrine clothed in excitement. Preaching is love's smile. Preaching is sin's greatest adversary. Preaching is the revival of broken dreams. Preaching is the sinner's best friend. Preaching is the saint's dinner. Preaching is genius with a halo. Preaching is fire in the pulpit that melts the ice in the pew.[4]

PREACH THE WORD

Preaching has always been a part of God's plan for communicating Truth. We must make His Word central to our worship. Praise, thanks, confession, proclamation, songs—these are all appropriate acts of worship, but a church built on programs or music alone is a church built on shifting sands. Preaching is the fundamental component of pastoral ministry.

Today, Seventh-day Adventists are renowned for orphanages, hospitals, and universities. But in the past, our defining characteristic was our preaching and distinct message.

It is sad to admit, but many of our preachers have become nothing more than second-rate psychologists, using the pulpit as a couch. Today, like never before, we need to return to the basics. We must recommit ourselves to honest, Bible-based preaching.

> "*Preaching is the delivering of meat, not strawberries.*"
> –HUGH LATIMER

As Seventh-day Adventists preachers, we must recognize our identity as the remnant church. Ours is not a generic protestant or evangelical message. God has given us a prophetic message for this special moment in earth's history. Let us proclaim His message to His church now.

We are a people of hope. A true understanding of Revelation 14:6, 7 leads to a spirit-filled, vibrant church pulsating with a sense of mission to share the gospel with the world. Jesus' return is a thrilling message. As preachers, we must help people prepare for it. As we preach of His return, let us also deliver messages designed to help people live victoriously until His return.

PRAYER POWER

Ask your church to hold you up in prayer. Ask for their prayers to help you commit yourself to the study of scripture rigorously, carefully, and earnestly. Ask for their prayers to help you open up to God's leading and to the understanding of His Word. Ask for their prayers to help you shepherd the church in the right direction (Acts 6:4; Ephesians 6:19-20). And, in turn, you must pray for church members who are called to preach and teach God's Word. Pray that your church commits to hearing God's Word so that your church's agenda will be increasingly shaped by God's agenda in scripture.

The church needs preachers to preach the whole truth, whether or not it is popular. In Isaiah's day, the people cried out, "See no more visions! . . . Give us no more visions of what is right! Tell us pleasant things prophesy illusions" (Isaiah 30:10). This attitude applies to the church today. People tend to reject what makes them uncomfortable. They want to hear things that affirm their lifestyles and make them feel good. Many pastors fall into the trap of pandering to their congregation in an effort to be liked.

Whom are you trying to please when you preach? You will never please everyone all the time. You must only strive to please God. You must preach messages that will disturb the comfortable and comfort the disturbed.

The Seventh-day Adventist Church has been given a precious message to be loudly proclaimed to the entire world. We are not commissioned to preach just any gospel, but the everlasting gospel. This means a wholistic understanding of the Bible. The everlasting gospel means God has been actively involved in our redemption since the beginning of time. Christ is present from the first pages of the Bible. The Old Testament anticipates His first advent. The New Testament chronicles His arrival, life, death, and above all, His advocacy on our behalf. Many preachers neglect these precious truths for the sake of *relevance*. Yet is there anything more relevant than what Christ is doing for us in heaven? Judgment has begun, a judgment that is "in favor of the saints" (Daniel 7:22, NKJ)! The good news of the gospel, the everlasting gospel, does not stop with a command to make disciples of all nations; it builds upon the revelations throughout the Bible. From Genesis to Revelation, God's Word proclaims the last stage of Christ's ministry before our redemption. Fleeing from such a task is not mere negligence; it is a sin. Proclaiming such a message demands preparation. No website can prepare a preacher as well as prayerful solitude before the Lord through the study of scripture.

LIFT UP CHRIST

A sermon cannot inspire love for Christ if there is no mention of Christ. Even if you are exhorting people on important practical matters, you have not preached a sermon until you speak of the beauty of Jesus. You have merely given a lesson on ethics.

> " Do not preach until you know what Christ is to you."
>
> –ELLEN G. WHITE

27

On the importance of always presenting Christ to the congregation, Ellen White says, "Christ crucified, Christ risen, Christ ascended into the heavens, Christ coming again, should so soften, gladden, and fill the mind of the minister that he will present these truths to the people in love and deep earnestness. The minister will then be lost sight of, and Jesus will be made manifest. Lift up Jesus, you that teach the people, lift Him up in sermon, in song, in prayer."[5]

Above all else, a sermon must inspire love for Christ. If you have not done this, your preaching has been in vain. While you may sincerely intend to inspire in your congregation a love for Christ, put your good intention to the test. Ask random church members what they got out of the sermon. If the answer does not reflect a greater appreciation and affection for Christ, you have failed your flock. "The important thing is that in every way, whether from false motives or true, Christ is preached. And because of this I rejoice" (Philippians 1:18).

LIVE WHAT YOU PREACH

There is much truth in the saying *I would rather see a sermon than hear one any day.* A pastor must be an example to his flock. Of course, perfection is an impossibility. Instead, we must be a model of constant seeking and surrender. When someone preaches with sincerity, people will see it—not only in the way he preaches, but also in the way he lives.

> " *Preach not because you have to say something, but because you have something to say."*
>
> –Richard Whitely

I love preaching! Few other activities bring me more joy than standing before God's people, delivering a message from His Word. I get passionate when seeing the change it brings about in peoples' lives. When I preach the Word faithfully and passionately, people transform into Christ-like disciples. And I change too!

THE PREPARATION

"Help me to remember that I am a prophet; not a promoter; not a religious manager—but a prophet," wrote Aiden Wilson

Tozer.[6] Effective preaching begins with preparation. And sermon preparation must always begin in the quiet presence of God.

If we are to proclaim God's Word to hungry and thirsty people, we must spend time in God's presence. Only then can we be prepared to represent Him. It is a great privilege to deliver God's message. As you preach, you become God's voice before His people.

William Culbertson said, "The sermon without the life is worthless, and the sermon without the Word is powerless."[7] The time spent alone in personal worship and Bible study is very important. There is a direct relationship between the efficacy of our preaching and the quality of our personal walk with God. You cannot attempt to feed others when your own soul hungers.

If our preaching is lacking, so are we. Powerful and effective sermons require time spent in prayer and study. Ask God to allow His message to flow through you.

> " *The devil will let a preacher prepare a sermon if it will keep him from preparing himself."*
> – VANCE HAVNER

Pastors in some denominations work other jobs during the week and pastor their churches on the weekend. Yet many of them manage to juggle both work responsibilities and accomplish remarkable works. Full-time pastors, then, should be more effective and accomplish more. Pastors need to invest time in such a way as to be ever prepared to preach good sermons.

PREACH CLEARLY

The Bible says "they read from the Book of the Law of God, making it clear and giving the meaning so that the people understood what was being read" (Nehemiah 8:8). Many pastors make a concerted effort to preach meaningful sermons. I have discovered my sermons become meaningful when I preach as though each sermon was my last. I remember on many occasions realizing, as I led in a funeral service, that the last sermon the deceased ever heard was mine from the previous Sabbath. This jarring reality compels me to focus on making every sermon I preach meaningful. Think about your church members who are living through difficult times and need encouragement or affirmation. When you preach, you are God's instrument to touch their lives in a very meaningful way.

It is a solemn moment when we present God's message to His people. We are stepping on holy ground. This truth inspires me to conclude each sermon with an appeal. I have seen many good preachers deliver good sermons. But often, they forget the importance of making an appeal. A sermon without an appeal is no more than a speech. It is like a salesman who shows off a new book, explains the importance of reading that book, and then fails to invite the client to buy it. No sermon, Bible study, or testimony should be concluded without a call to Christ. Why make an appeal? Because it's biblical. It's logical. And it urges people to commit themselves to truth.

Ellen White affirms "many times minds are impressed with tenfold more force by personal appeals than by any other kind of labor."[8] Power is lost when a preacher neglects this special moment at the end of the sermon. The lives of many depend upon this moment. "There are souls in every congregation who are hesitating, almost persuaded to be wholly for God. The decision is being made for time and for eternity; but it is too often the case that the minister has not the spirit and power of the message of truth in his own heart, hence no direct appeals are made to those souls that are trembling in the balance."[9]

> *Do you expect people to come to Christ every time you preach?"*
> – CHARLES H. SPURGEON

The famous preacher Dwight L. Moody once failed to make an appeal after his Sunday sermon the week of the great Chicago fire. Hundreds died in that tragic incident, among those many who had been in his church.[10] He later called it "the biggest mistake I made in all my years of ministry."

CONTEXTUALIZE YOUR MESSAGE

For our message to gain an audience, we must contextualize it. We must communicate in a culturally appropriate, effective, and relevant way. We must ensure that our congregation can relate to and understand our message. The world has changed. If we refuse to acknowledge this in our preaching, the gospel will get left behind.

Too often we say *I want to make the Bible relevant.* There is no need for this. God has already given us a message that is relevant in every cultural context. Our job is to present it in ways that help the listener see that relevancy. We do so by taking them to scripture. Just as Jesus did, we must preach in a way that people can best understand and respond to the gospel message.

> " *Actors speak of things imaginary as if they were real; preachers speak of things real as if they were imaginary."*
>
> –THOMAS BETTERTON

Our aim is to preach sermons that are culturally relevant, while remaining grounded in biblical principles. To achieve this, focus on these questions:

Why is this important?
How does this relate to me?
What does the Bible say about it?
How can I apply this knowledge to my life?

Instead of:
The Bible says this, so it must be important, and I should do it.[11]

DYNAMIC PREACHING

Are you a dynamic or boring preacher? My seminary professor used to say, "Many people will be in heaven, saved by their patient endurance of boring preachers." I hope no one in your congregation describes your preaching in the following way: "I never see my preacher's eyes, however bright they shine; for when he prays, he closes his; and when he preaches, he closes mine!" (Raymond Barber)

There is a story that further illustrates this: A man went to see his doctor about his snoring. The doctor asked, "Does your snoring disturb your wife?"

"My wife?" he replied, "Why, it disturbs the whole congregation during the sermon!"

When a church gathers to hear a sermon, there are listeners of different ages and varied education levels, vocations, and backgrounds. It is the preacher's task to discover a method to get the message through to all of them. While everyone may not be interested in every subject, any subject can be made interesting if presented the right way. So how do we meet this challenge?

Lack of motivation is a chief contributor to boring sermons. Pastors love delivering urgent, timely messages. These are the sermons that excite us. Unfortunately, the occasion to deliver such a sermon doesn't always present itself. Sometimes, Sabbath comes and we are left searching. It is easy to just preach a filler sermon— something to fulfill our obligation and earn our salary. But, be warned. Your congregation will not be fooled by false sincerity.

A preacher must be on fire with his message. This passion infused in his words will permeate throughout the congregation. And they will connect with it.

I challenge you to become a dynamic preacher and, through your ministry, become a blessing to those around you. Should you find this daunting, remember "success means being the best. Excellence means being your best. Success, to many, means being better than everyone else. Excellence means being better tomorrow than you were yesterday. Success means exceeding the achievements of other people. Excellence means matching your practice with your potential."[12]

CAN YOU BE A GOOD PASTOR WITHOUT BEING AN EFFECTIVE PREACHER?

Questions for reflection, consideration, or discussion:

1. How do you, personally, define a "good preacher?"
2. Why should preaching be the primary responsibility of a pastor?
3. Why are preachers fleeing the pulpit?
4. What should you do to avoid preaching boring sermons?
5. What does it truly mean to preach the Word of God and lift up Christ?

Chapter 3

A SPIRITUAL LEADER

Leadership is essential to effective pastoral ministry. It has the power to direct people towards good or evil, success or failure.

There are many pastors with great ideas, who fail to execute them. Good ideas alone do not make you an effective leader. True leadership is the confluence of motives, ideas, and actions.

The Bible gives us several models of good leadership. We see the far-reaching influence of godly leaders such as Moses, Samuel, and David. They were by no means infallible. But they accomplished great things for their people and their God. The Bible also mentions bad leaders such as Saul, Ahab, and Manasseh. These men show how leaders can use their power to influence people toward evil.

Jesus once said, "Leave them; they are blind guides. If the blind lead the blind, both will fall into a pit" (Matthew 15:14). A lack of proper leadership can lead people into trouble. Conversely, leadership that is in agreement with God's principles has the power to deliver people from trouble.

> *Don't tell people how to do things, tell them what to do and let them surprise you with their results."*
> –GEORGE S. PATTON

As Jesus evaluated the church in His day, "He had compassion on them, because they were harassed and helpless, like sheep without a shepherd" (Matthew 9:36). He recognized Israel's terrible leadership and wept. The people lacked the leadership that they so desperately needed.

As in Jesus' time, the world church today faces a leadership crisis. People are in dire need of spiritual leaders–not just leaders, but *spiritual* leaders. And I believe God is raising up a new generation of spiritual leaders that will reach the world for Jesus Christ.

LEADERSHIP CATEGORIES

Leadership can be divided into two categories.

Natural leadership. Some people are natural-born leaders. If you put ten people in a room, you could easily identify the natural leader within a few minutes. These people inherently take on leadership roles.

Spiritual leadership. A spiritual leader is one who wants to be led by the Spirit of God. He not only leads others, but also allows God to lead him. He allows God to instill in him a new heart, life, motivation, desire, vision, and values.

A SPIRIT-FILLED LEADER

A pastor must be a spiritual leader. Skill and experience are both important traits and should not be minimized. But being Spirit-filled and Spirit-led are the most essential and important qualities for pastoral leadership. True power in ministry springs from spirituality, which, in turn, comes from a personal encounter with God.

Church leadership is a call to spirituality. Spirituality should be a pre-requisite for all church leaders. Leadership should be seen as a great privilege, not a daunting responsibility. Your personal relationship with God must come first. Spirituality must be developed privately, before you can have any meaningful public influence.

The Bible teaches us that God seeks out those willing to commit to Him—people after His own heart, able to lead others (Jeremiah 3:15). These spiritual leaders must couple their knowledge with moral and spiritual fitness. Despite our recognition of personal spirituality as our first priority, the grind of professional ministry can take its toll. It is easy to become dispensers of truth without the actions to make it credible. Brent Filson says, "You can boost your leadership skills and hence your career by understanding this one thing that most leaders miss: great leadership incorporates a spiritual dimension."[1]

Spiritual leadership is shepherding God's flock where He desires. It means taking initiative, applying His methods, and relying on His power. The goal of spiritual leadership is that people come to know God and to glorify Him in all they do.

To become the leaders we ought to be, we must develop people rather than dictate plans. Spiritual leadership should not only direct, but also transform. You can get people to do what you want, but if their hearts are not changed, you have not led them spiritually. You have not taken them to where God wants them to be.[2]

A spiritual leader is a person of prayer. Time spent in prayer is absolutely essential to an authentic pastor's daily life. Though it should be a part of every Christian's life, it is especially true in the life of the pastor. Prayer is more than a simple ritual. If the bulk of a pastor's prayer time transpires at meal times, bedtime, while visiting church members, and on Sabbath before preaching, he is doomed to fail. He cannot stay filled with the Spirit without constant prayer in his life. We must realize and express our total dependence upon God. Without Him, we can do nothing.

> *You can't lead anyone else further than you have gone yourself."*
> –GENE MAUCH

Every pastor should keep a list of the members of his congregation. Several times a week, if not daily, he should go through the names; think about each one; and pray for God to guide, protect, and bless them.

There are those who are physically, emotionally, and spiritually sick. God often places a burden on my heart to pray for someone, even if I don't know of any specific problem they are experiencing. Paul told the church at Corinth, "Even if you had ten thousand guardians in Christ, you do not have many fathers" (I Corinthians 4:15). The same holds true today. There are many preachers who teach about Jesus Christ, but very few who love their flock as a pastor should. There is a major difference between a good preacher and a good pastor. A good pastor does more than preach a good sermon; he loves each member of the church as if they were his own children.

Pastoral prayer does not end with church issues. Prayer should extend to all aspects of our lives. A consecrated pastor must spend much time in prayer, if he is to live a victorious life in the kingdom of heaven while he lives here in this world.[3]

A spiritual leader must be a person of "vital piety." Although preaching is an important aspect of the pastoral ministry, Ellen White reminds us that "to minister, comprehends much more than mere preaching. In order to fulfill this sacred and important work freighted with eternal interests, the minister must be a man of vital piety, or his labors will not be accepted of God. He must be a man who will not have an exalted opinion of himself, or of his own ability, but who will lose a sense of his importance in the exalted view he has of the matchless mercy and love of Jesus Christ. He then has a close walk with God. His life of piety and true holiness which he carries with him wherever he goes, and which is interwoven in all his works, makes him a successful and efficient worker."[4]

A pastor must realize that his church's spiritual life is directly tied to his own. If your church requires revival, you must be revived. Unless change occurs within, you cannot affect change. No doubt you remember the adage that everything rises and falls on leadership. This is especially true in the spirituality of the church.

A good pastor should center his ministry on the person and work of Christ, whose character he must reflect. A pastor is to be an example to the flock God has given him. His power comes from God, who called him, not from his own personality or abilities. His life should command as his tongue persuades.

> *You do not lead by hitting people over the head. That's assault, not leadership."*
>
> –Dwight D. Eisenhower

A spiritual leader must lead with love. There is no room for unkindness or force in church leadership. Spiritual leaders must not perform their duties arrogantly nor rule the church with tyranny. They are not to have a highhanded, autocratic rule. Yet they must lead.

THE PURPOSE OF SPIRITUAL LEADERSHIP

The main purpose of spiritual leadership is twofold.

Glorify God. People tend to recognize leaders who build bigger buildings or increase fundraising—leaders whose motivations are fame and popularity. But a spiritual leader has only one motivation—to bring glory to God.

As a spiritual leader, you can do great things—promote church programs, mobilize people into missionary activities, give Bible studies, lead evangelistic crusades, baptize thousands of people. But remember, the true purpose of ministry is to bring glory and honor to God. Let that truth be the motivation for your work. When God evaluates spiritual leaders, He does not focus on accomplishments. He looks at your motives. Many different things can motivate a leader. But a spiritual leader's main motive is always to bring glory to God!

Serve others. We must remember that Jesus came to serve. It is very easy to slip into glorifying ourselves instead of God, serving ourselves instead of others. We must always examine our motivation as spiritual leaders. Our prayer should be *God, I want to glorify you and serve others*. Ask yourself, *why am I doing this?* We must ensure that our actions have the right motivation.

PRACTICING SPIRITUAL LEADERSHIP

Spiritual leadership is evidenced during times of conflict. The church is no stranger to conflict. When congregations bicker over doctrines, worship style, or personnel, it is a time for pastors and elders to demonstrate spiritual leadership by promoting peace and reconciliation, rather than publicly making negative comments.

Spiritual leadership needs to be trustworthy. People need to be able to disclose their problems and concerns without fear of private information being made public. Without trust and integrity, it is impossible to build a good ministry.

Spiritual leadership shows integrity. Church leaders are looked upon for guidance. Their lives need to be above reproach so their advice and counsel will be taken seriously. This is not to say that church leaders are perfect. Rather, they try to practice what they preach, without hypocrisy.

Spiritual leadership expresses mercy to others without being judgmental. When people make mistakes, they need to be counseled and helped—not condemned. A person who offers spiritual leadership at these times should address the issue and help find a solution.[5]

A SPIRITUAL LEADER

Spiritual leadership demands a person of character. Character is extremely important in any kind of leadership, but especially so in spiritual leaders. If you lose your reputation, you lose your leadership. Our behavior is our message. When the apostle Paul speaks about spiritual qualification in his writings, he speaks of character issues. If you are going to be a spiritual leader, you have to be a person of character.

BE THE BEST YOU CAN BE
The best leaders practice what they preach in all things, regardless of importance. The opportunities to practice good leadership are abundant. It is never too late to start developing these skills.

Be optimistic. Spiritual leaders are optimistic, because they know God is in control. Leaders don't let themselves become discouraged by circumstances. When they see imperfection in the church, they see an opportunity to build a better congregation.[6]

Be tactful. Paul said in Colossians 4:5-6, "Be wise in the way you act toward outsiders; make the most of every opportunity. Let your conversation be always full of grace, seasoned with salt, so that you know how to answer everyone." Proverbs tells us, "Like apples of gold in settings of silver is a ruling rightly given" (25:11).

> *"Tact is the intelligence of the heart."*
> –Unknown

Remember that leaders aim to change hearts, not just to finish a job. A tactful leader knows the difference between saying *Your foot is too big for this shoe* and *This shoe is too small for your foot.*[7] A tactful leader possesses the grace that wins the confidence of his people.[8]

Be a trainer. Competent leaders must be trainers. Training is integral to any organization, including God's church. Many pastors spend a lot of time in sermon preparation and little time actually training their church members. Ellen White suggests that pastors spend more time educating than preaching.[9] She also affirms, "The greatest help that can be given our people is to teach them to work for God, and to depend on Him, not on the ministers."[10] When there is no training in the church, the results will be:

- Shortage of church workers
- Lack of production
- Stagnancy in personnel
- Understaffed departments
- Decrease in volunteers

As church leaders, we cannot forget that election does not mean qualification. Training is necessary for all. When we delegate, we assume the responsibility of training. We need more training programs in the local church.

In a church leadership study, it was discovered that when ten members in volunteer ministry are well trained and committed to church service, they are equivalent to a full-time pastor.[11] In other words, a hundred trained people are the equivalent of ten pastors working together.

Unfortunately, we do not invest enough in the training of new leaders. As a result, we hear "If that elder dies, we have nobody to replace him" or "If that family moves to another city, our church will close its doors." This lack of training is a sad reality that we must remedy.

Be a dreamer. Dreaming of a better future is the answer to restlessness. As leaders, we must not be satisfied with the present. We cannot allow ourselves, or our churches, to become stagnant. We must always be searching for ways to improve, regardless of how dire the circumstances may seem. 2 Kings 6:15-17 tells us the story of Elisha and his servant. They were trapped in the city of Dothan surrounded by Assyrians.

It seemed hopeless. When his servant cried out in dismay, Elisha prayed, "Open his eyes, Lord, so that he may see." When God opened the eyes of the young man, he saw horses and chariots of fire standing by their side.

> *To accomplish great things, we must not only act, but also dream; not only plan, but also believe."*
>
> –ANATOLE FRANCE

Spiritual leaders can see the power of God overshadow the problems of the future. They see the sovereign power of God triumph in the midst of seemingly overwhelming opposition.

Joel 2:28 tells us that old men will dream dreams. How sad it is to see so many older people assume that they can sit back and turn over the creativity to the youth. It is tragic when age makes a man jaded instead of increasingly creative. Every new church, every new ministry, every institution, every endeavor is the result of vision and opportunity seized.[12]

Be a lover. Spiritual leaders love their people. Through their words and attitudes, they express joy in serving those around them. Spiritual leaders love their people. Through their words and attitudes, they express joy in serving those around them. How do we learn to love? Start at home. Paul says in Ephesians 5:25, "Husbands, love your wives." Such a simple directive, yet it is so often overlooked. There is danger in sacrificing balance in your personal life for your ministry. What good is it to grow your congregation, yet lose your marriage? We need leaders who value the expression of love.

Write your wife romantic cards. Buy her flowers. Take a day off and spend it with her alone. Don't put her down; compliment her instead. Look her in the eyes when you talk. Put down the papers. Turn off the television. Help her with the dishes. Throw her a party. Love her! If you don't, all your success as a leader will mean nothing compared to your failure at home.[13] Loving your wife will help you better love your church.

A GOOD LEADER

A good leader understands the hopes, dreams, and aspirations of his people.

A good leader believes in transparent honesty and accountability.

A good leader works toward the greater good of his people.

A good leader shares in the power of the people to choose.

A good leader is tactful, frugal, responsible, and responsive.

A good leader does today what others are thinking of tomorrow.

A good leader is not afraid of mistakes, no matter how minute they may be.

A good leader paves the way, even for generations unborn.

A good leader has an avalanche of courage even to offend allies and friends in the course of justice.

A good leader is judged by the content of his character and integrity of intent.

A good leader, above all, is a good follower.[14]

CAN YOU BE A GOOD PASTOR WITHOUT BEING A SPIRITUAL LEADER?

Questions for reflection, consideration, or discussion:

1. How do you define a spiritual leader?
2. What may change in my leadership if everything must be done for the glory of God?
3. What are the main qualities you most value in a leader?
4. Why is integrity so important in church leadership?
5. In which aspects should you improve your leadership and how can you get there?

A SPIRITUAL LEADER

Chapter 4

A PRAYERFUL PERSON

If anyone needs to pray faithfully and fervently, it is the pastor. By accepting the Lord's call into the ministry, we agree to live in a world of unfinished tasks. We are called to live beyond ourselves. It is impossible to live this life and accomplish our tasks through our own strength. We must develop strong prayer lives or we will not survive. It is as simple as that. We must realize and express our total dependence upon God. Without Him, we can do nothing.

The pastor who depends on his own strength, who preaches and serves from his own resources, will soon find himself weak, discouraged, and ready to quit. No one has the wisdom for all of life's decisions. No one has the patience to overcome all the problems encountered. No one has the time for all the tasks, energy for all the meetings, inspiration for all the messages, and enough compassion for all the people who need him. Being a pastor doesn't change these truths. Pray or quit. That is the choice.

Pastors are leaders of God's household. They must remember that Jesus said God's house shall be called a house of prayer (Matthew 21:13). He did not call it a house of preaching or a house of praise. He called it a house of prayer. Preaching and praise can never really begin, or have any effect, without a foundation of fervent prayer. Preaching, praise, and worship must be preceded by prayer.

THE ROOT OF DISSATISFACTION

Prayer is sadly absent in the hearts, minds, and studies of many pastors. They seem to think prayer is either unimportant and undeserving of a place in their ministry or there is simply no room for prayer among their many responsibilities. As pastors, we must prioritize prayer. It is our first line of defense against dissatisfaction as well as the primary task of a pastor.

In the book *My House Shall Be Called a House of Prayer*, Steve Loopstra shares his personal experience after graduating from seminary. He loved preaching and teaching the Word of God. But as he began his ministry, he discovered that people expected more. They expected plans, programs, and results. He felt these expectations not only from the church members, but also from the leadership in his denomination. He began to look for ways to promote church growth, evangelism, and discipleship. His ministry became focused on working hard and attaining results. His denominational leaders emphasized results, and he saw other pastors doing the same. And he accepted it as the ministerial lifestyle. However, he felt a growing disquiet in his heart. He was getting tired of the endless parade of programs. He discovered that the dissatisfaction he was feeling stemmed from his growing distance from God. He began to realize that his prayer life deepened as he learned to view prayer as part of his love relationship with a God who was actively seeking him out.[1] Loopstra's experience mirrors that of many other pastors.

Ellen White says, "No work for the church should take precedence over communion with God. There is nothing more needed in the work than the practical results of communion with God. We should show by our daily lives that we have peace and rest in God. His

> *Prayer makes the man; prayer makes the preacher; prayer makes the pastor."*
>
> –E. M. Bounds

peace in the heart will shine forth in the countenance. It will give to the voice a persuasive power. Communion with God will impart a moral elevation to the character and to the entire course of action. Men will take knowledge of us, as of the first disciples, that we have been with Jesus. This will impart to the minister's labors a power even greater than that which comes from the influence of his preaching. Of this power he must not allow himself to be deprived. Communion with God through prayer and the study of His word must not be neglected, for here is the source of his strength. No work for the church should take precedence of this."[2]

A prayerful pastor is one who spends time in the presence of the Father, seeking Him, and hearing His desire for the church. A prayerful pastor finds direction not from the latest seminar, but through prayer.

As pastors, prayer sustains us. Ministry rests on the spiritual condition of its leaders. Their devotion to Christ, and what flows from that devotion, determines the efficacy of their ministry. For ministry to be blessed and effective, we must maintain a healthy relationship with our Lord and hold each other accountable. We must not independently go about our work; we must depend on our Lord Jesus Christ and on one another. Christianity is not a solo sport or a spectator sport; it is a team effort in which we form one body and one force for one Kingdom.

A SENSELESS SHEPHERD

If we are too busy for prayer, how can we be effective in God's service? Remember, we cannot do the Lord's work unless we are the Lord's people. We must begin with our own spiritual condition—with our relationship with Christ. We must nurture our own growth before we can effectively minister to others. And to grow, we must be on our knees. If you don't think you can do this, perhaps you should find another job. My advice is to get right with God.

The prophet Jeremiah gives us insight into pastors who do not prosper in their ministerial work—"The shepherds are senseless and do not inquire of the LORD; so they do not prosper and all their flock is scattered" (Jeremiah 10:21). As we read Jeremiah's words we can begin to better understand that being a prayerful pastor is essential in developing our relationship with God. It means learning how to listen for His voice and His direction.

Charles Spurgeon said, "If you as ministers are not very prayerful, you are much to be pitied. If, in the future, you shall be called to sustain pastorates, large or small, if you become lax in secret devotion, not only will you need to be pitied, but your people also; and, in addition to that, you shall be blamed, and the day cometh in which you shall be ashamed and confounded."[3]

BECOMING A PRAYING PASTOR

Effective ministry is impossible without prayer at its center. We cannot meet the approval of God without prayer. How can we receive His blessings when we leave Him out of the loop? If we do not include God in our lives, how can we serve Him?

Our relationship with others is a reflection of our relationship with God. This applies whether we are leaders, new Christians, or lay members. If we have a poor relationship with God, then our human, interpersonal relations will be compromised as well. When our relationship with our Lord is built on prayer, then our relationships with one another will flourish as well. This is a must for all Christians, essential for leaders, and imperative for the pastor.

Charles Bridges says, "My brethren—a pastor who does not pray, who does not love prayer, does not belong to that Church, which 'prays without ceasing'; he is a dry and barren tree, which cumbers the Lord's ground; he is the enemy, and not the father of his people; he is a stranger, who has usurped the pastor's place, and to whom the salvation of the flock is indifferent. Wherefore, my brethren, be faithful to prayer, and your functions will be more useful, your people more holy, your labours will prove much sweeter, and the Church's evils will diminish."[4]

> "*Prayer must be our first resource, not our last resort.*"
> –HENRY BLACKABY

How do you transform from a pastor who prays to a prayerful pastor? Here are some suggestions gleaned from my own journey:

Ask God to search your heart and reveal the true state of your prayer life. Ask the Lord to lead you into a more meaningful prayer life. Be honest with yourself. Have you relegated prayer to simply one of many tools in your pastoral toolbox? Or is it the guiding force in your decision-making? Deepen your relationship with Him. Have you been skimming along, allowing sermon preparation to replace your personal devotion time? Or are you feeding your soul and seeking God above all else?

Develop an ability to discern and hear the voice of the Lord. Throughout history God has spoken to His people. Listen through the Word, and through the Spirit who dwells within you. Learn to recognize His voice.

Seek out the intercessors in your church and ask them to pray for you. You might be surprised how delighted they would be to pray for you to become a prayerful pastor.

God calls His people to experience the power and privilege of prayer.

PRAYER LIST

Every pastor needs a church directory. Several times a week, if not daily, he should go through the names and pray for each member. He should ask for God's guidance, protection and blessing for each one. We need to pray specifically for each person He has put under our care. Remember, "as a minister, no man has a right to preach to a crowd that he has not prayed for."[5]

THE IMPORTANCE OF A PRAYER LIFE

Prayer is the foundation of all religious life. It must be evident in our lives and ministry. Ignoring the importance of prayer eventually weakens our ministry and causes us to stumble on our journey.

Prayer, in its most basic form, is communication with God. Prayer leads us to dependence upon Him. A person completely devoted to God proclaims *I am nothing and God is supreme.* Prayer produces faith. Claiming to have faith without prayer is like dinner without food, like a wedding without bride, like a storm without rain. A vibrant prayer life leads us to confession, conviction, and righteous decisions. Prayer leads us to stand firm in Jesus and to a victorious life. Seeking our own desires only leads to a life of dissatisfaction. We must aim to lead a victorious life. Allow God's presence to guide you and help you fulfill His purpose.

Without prayer, God's servant is like a ship without a sail, ignorant of God's direction. Frustration and disappointment replace victory and confidence. A mighty prayerful servant knows the direction in which God is leading him and is all the more useful.

CULTIVATING A PERSONAL PRAYER LIFE

The biggest enemy to the pastor's prayer life is his own lack of discipline. It is easy to get caught up in the same busyness that infects everyone. Every day is a battle for the use of your time. Without fervent prayer, the pastor becomes spiritually impotent and weak. He must be disciplined and refuse to allow anyone or anything to come between him and fervent prayer with God.

> *Don't pray when it rains if you don't pray when the sun shines."*
>
> –SATCHEL PAIGE

When I make prayer a priority, my ministry flourishes. When I forget prayer or place it on the back-burner, I am stressed, inefficient, and ineffective. Prayer is a source of strength in ministry. It unleashes the power of God in us and through us unto others.

Here is a sample prayer plan for pastors.

1. *Cultivate a rich prayer life.* Make prayer a priority. Rearrange your schedule; find time. Have others keep you accountable. Do what it takes to pray and do so with joy, gratitude, and sincerity. Embrace and apply the other disciplines of the Christian faith—fasting and meditation. While there will be dry spells, effort and passion must be present. Our communication with our Lord Jesus Christ is based on giving ourselves completely to Him, because He has first done so for us. This is why we serve Him. We say that He is our Lord; thus, we must live, work, and respond accordingly.

2. *Have a prayer partner.* A pastoral prayer partner is someone in whom the pastor can safely confide in. God calls some church members to become prayer partners for their pastor.

They should meet regularly as a team. If meeting in person is difficult to schedule, they can pray for each other by phone. The pastor would do well to be surrounded by the prayers of his church members as he pastors in these difficult times.

An effective personal prayer life should include:
- A regular time and place.
- Small but sustainable prayer time (5-15 minutes). You will find that your prayer time increases as you are faithful in daily prayer.
- Your Bible, a notebook, and a pen. The Bible helps you base your prayer requests on God's Word. The notebook will help

you keep track of prayer requests and the impressions that come from God.

- Time to worship God before you begin your prayer time.
- Time to listen to God before you make your requests.
- Organized prayer requests. Start with your most personal needs and work your way out to the needs of others: family members, prayer partners, church members, missionaries, church leaders, and world needs.

Now that you have read the prayer guidelines, why not take a few minutes to put them into practice right now?

You cannot take a break from prayer. The Bible tells us to "pray without ceasing" (1 Thessalonians 5:17, NKJV). You do not take a break from oxygen, food, or water. Through prayer, we grow and flourish. If we become thoughtless and careless with our prayer life, we will be thoughtless and careless in our interactions with those around us. Our spiritual priorities are our life priorities. Do not neglect your prayer just as our Lord does not neglect us. Let us go before His presence with confidence and the authority He gives us. Then, we can be the people of His work and will.[6]

IS IT POSSIBLE TO BE A GOOD PASTOR WITHOUT HAVING A FERVENT PRAYER LIFE?

Questions for reflection, consideration, or discussion:

1. What is the difference between a *pastor who prays* and a *prayerful pastor*?
2. Can lack of a prayer life cause ministerial frustrations?
3. Explain why the shepherds in Jeremiah's time were senseless (Jeremiah 10:21)?
4. What can you improve in your life and ministry if more time is spent in prayer?
5. What are the benefits of having a prayer list and a prayer partner?

A PRAYERFUL PERSON

Chapter 5

A RELATIONSHIP-ORIENTED PASTOR

Why do some pastors flourish in their ministry while others, with superior theological and practical training, fail? Why do insignificant events often affect people in significant ways? Why do people leave vibrant, exciting churches while others remain loyal to those with very little to offer? What makes the difference? Relationships. Pastors with strong personal skills, who work to establish healthy relationships, thrive almost anywhere they go. Pastors without these skills can struggle, despite engaging in the same practices as their colleagues. A good pastor needs good relationship skills.

THE IMPORTANCE OF BUILDING GOOD RELATIONSHIPS

Quality relationships are one of the keys to successful pastoral ministry. Leadership is not a matter of using skills and implementing practices. Nor is it about being right all the time. Leadership is about nurturing good, strong relationships.

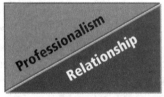

The 50/50 Principle

When I was invited to work in the South American Division Ministerial Association, I was afraid of the enormous challenges that accompanied the job. I asked a veteran pastor and friend of mine for some advice. On a piece of paper he drew a rectangle and said, "This is your whole ministry." He then crossed a line from one corner to the other and said, "It is important to understand 50% of your ministry is professionalism and the other 50% is relationships. You can be less professional and succeed. But if you are not relationship-oriented, you will certainly run into problems in your ministry." I have found this to be true. Administrators in our church prefer to work with those with people skills rather than with more qualified professionals without people skills. It is much easier to work with them as a team. They are more flexible and open-minded. Relationship-building is a skill we can learn to develop. It starts by praying for good relationships wherever we are.

> **66** *The easiest kind of relationship for me is with 10,000 people. The hardest is with one."*
>
> –JOAN BAEZ

Relationships should be a concern for every pastor, even those whose main emphasis is teaching or administration. A gifted preacher can draw closer to his people by engaging them during a sermon. But, a pastor whose strength is not preaching can still build strong relationships and a sense of community. None of us can be good at everything, but our relationships are the cement that holds it all together.

RELATING TO CHURCH MEMBERS

In order to minister to people, we must know them. Good relationships motivate people, open hearts, and bring us closer together. In my ministry, I have discovered some ways to build good relationships with church members:

Be available and accessible. Have you heard the expression that pastors are invisible during the week and impossible to find on Sabbath? Greeting your members at the door is a great way to be accessible. Develop a ministry at the door before and after the service. Just be there and be available. There is nothing as nice as a cheerful word of greeting! Smile at them. Call people by name. Be friendly and helpful. As a pastor, you must show genuine interest and respect for people.

Keeping regular office hours can also help you connect with your congregation. Make sure you have a set time and place to attend to church members' needs during the week. Communicate through the church bulletin that you are available, and those who would like to talk can make an appointment with the church secretary. Be creative, and find the best way to be accessible to your congregation.

Often, while trying to be more available and accessible to church members, we run into difficulties. What if someone takes more time than scheduled? I often wrestle with this issue in my own ministry. I want to be available. But at the same time, I sometimes must ask myself *Where am I most needed in the church?*

> *If it is possible, as far as it depends on you, live at peace with everyone."*
> —ROMANS 12:18

As their pastor, the congregation needs me to be prepared, to nourish them spiritually with God's Word on Sabbath and throughout the week. This requires me to put in adequate prayer and study time. Unfortunately, I cannot always be available as much as some individuals would like. I have had to make some difficult decisions in limiting my visitation and counseling in order to leave enough time to work in other areas.

Church members often fail to recognize that their pastors have time limitations. As a pastor you may need to help them recognize this by establishing limits. Do not allow a church member to monopolize your time or agenda. You are a pastor of all your church members, not just a few. Pastors can end up spending 80% of their time with 20% of their church members. This should not be the case.

In dealing with this issue, I decided not to meet with a person for more than three consecutive counseling sessions. In the case of sickness or bereavement, after the initial visit, I involve my elders in follow-up visits to express our love and concern.

Build relationships. It takes a great deal of energy to build relationships. As a leader, you have other responsibilities that require a large amount of energy, including leading itself. But, when you invest in relationships with the people you lead, you are building a network that can provide encouragement, inspiration, and support during the good and bad times. Relationships are reciprocal. Maintain a positive attitude towards others, and they will do the same.

Be loving. Over the years, I've ordained many pastors. As part of this process, I have seen how some church members evaluate them. In some situations, they didn't even like their pastors and were even rude to them. Though not all members will love or even like you as a pastor, you still have the responsibility to love them all.

Jesus said, "Love one another. As I have loved you, so you must love one another. By this everyone will know that you are my disciples, if you love one another" (John 13:34-35). I have heard some pastors describe their members in unloving ways. I have also heard lay people describe how their pastors have treated them unkindly. This is something that you cannot disguise. You may lie and tell them that you love them. But sooner or later, they will know the truth. You can preach at them all you want, but you will not be permitted to pastor them if they do not feel loved.

> "When you look for the good in others, you discover the best in yourself."
> –MARTIN WALSH

Sadly, some churches have pastors that do not genuinely love their people. Words are important. But, they only ring true when accompanied by appropriate actions. Church members appreciate a pastor more when they see actions affirming the words of affection.

Be respectful. Leadership and respect are earned. These attributes are never granted because of name or position. They are earned rights. One earns the right to lead by providing good leadership. One earns respect by loving and serving people. A leader who loves and serves will be readily followed. A failure to respect and love people is a fatal flaw in any ministry.

People in the church will readily forgive a pastor's small faults when the pastor truly loves them. Conversely, I have seen people magnify small faults when affection is absent. Their list of faults seemed unimportant until they mentioned the big one—*Our minister doesn't love us*. After that, ministry is impossible.

A mean, ugly spirit of criticism pervades our culture. This same worldly attitude can sometimes trickle into the church. We must not allow it. Remember: "they will know we are Christians by our love."

RELATING TO FELLOW LEADERS

A pastor maintains many different kinds of relationships. His relationship with church elders, deacons, and other leaders are especially important. When there are strains in this area, a great amount of the church's energy is wasted. They will probably endure sleepless nights and the pastor's wife will most likely suffer the most. For your happiness and effectiveness within the church, as well as harmony at home, take time to develop strong relationships.

Meeting regularly with your church leaders can significantly help in relationship-building. You can meet in the church or in the home of one of the elders, along with wives and families. Feel free to discuss issues of common interest. But remember, this is not a business meeting; it is fellowship.

Start regular elder's retreats. This will allow you devoted time to plan and evaluate the church program. Cultivate a habit of showing appreciation for your church leaders and those involved in church activities. I try to include all the elders in the decision-making process. This makes them feel that we are moving ahead together. I do not want them to be yes men. Working as a team is very beneficial.

Churches occasionally have a member in leadership who resists the direction of the pastor and the whole board. If this occurs, love him. Do not try to undermine him. Publicly show appreciation for that particular member. Often the source of the problem is nothing more than miscommunication or a personal issue. Never take sides. Instead, encourage unity.

Interacting with church staff. It is important to cultivate good relationships with church staff—other pastors, secretaries, or interns. Good communication is key in these relationships. I tried to maintain good relationships with the church staff by keeping in contact with them through staff meetings every other week. We share devotional time, pray together, and share information about the ministry.

> *Be loyal to your boss, your company, and your co-workers. Someone is always listening."*
> –BRIAN TRACY

As church leaders, this practice often helps us avoid misunderstandings. I remember one member who came to my two associate pastors and me, separately. She asked us all the same question.

And all three of us gave her the same answer. This is because we had spoken of this particular issue beforehand. If we were not on the same page, we would have caused confusion.

MAKING AND KEEPING GOOD FRIENDS

Pastors seem to have a natural need for friends, and with good reason. Friends make life more enjoyable. They relieve feelings of loneliness. They can even help reduce stress and improve your health. Good friends are especially helpful in times of personal difficulty. Good friends and supporters can make all the difference.

We all need to be surrounded by the warm, cheerful presence of friends and loved ones. However, many pastors and their families find it difficult to establish and maintain close relationships. This is partly because we are often on the go. Fostering friendships and relationships require investments over long periods of time. And as clergy, this is often time we do not have.

Pastors can be some of the loneliest men. They can find themselves in unhealthy relationships where their wives are their only friends and counselors. I believe a pastor's wife should be his best friend, but not his only friend.

Proverbs 27:6 reads, "Wounds from a friend can be trusted, but an enemy multiplies kisses." Some friends are closer to the heart, some more superficial. But they are all useful. If you are a pastor without close friendships, I urge you to seek them out. They may keep you in ministry for the long haul. And your wife will thank you.

> *There is no conversation more boring than the one where everybody agrees.*
>
> –MICHEL DE MONTAIGNE

DO'S AND DON'TS IN RELATIONSHIPS

Here are some practical and important do's and don'ts to help you as you relate to others.

- DO smile; it costs nothing and is always appreciated!
- DON'T ignore people, even when you do not want to talk; be friendly when someone says "Hello!" It is not about how you feel; it is about how you portray yourself.

- DO make people feel important. Make each person feel special.
- DON'T brag. No one likes a person who is full of himself. Be an honest and humble person. It is far better that people find out about your achievements and abilities from sources other than yourself.
- DO have a sense of humor. Laugh and people will laugh with you.
- DON'T always discuss your problems and troubles; you will soon find yourself alone! We all have problems and need help; be discerning about knowing when to ask for help.
- DO encourage people. Tell others what you like about them or something they are doing well. Encouragement is the fuel that moves the engine of the church.
- DON'T criticize or cut people down including yourself! There is a difference between humbleness and a self-demeaning attitude.
- DO have an interest in many things. Be an interesting person and people will be interested in you.
- DON'T grab the best, biggest, and most for yourself; give others the best.
- DO meet strangers, although it may be difficult. You can make new friends by being friendly to someone you do not know.
- DON'T make fun of others when they make a mistake. Be the first to go to them with encouragement.
- DO help others when they have a problem and share what you have with them. We are to be the people who give attention.
- DON'T have a bad temper or be an angry person looking for an argument or a fight. Temperance is far better than temper!
- DO look good, clean, neat, and well-groomed. It was Benjamin Franklin who said, "Cleanliness is next to godliness."
- DO keep confidentiality. If someone tells you something, keep it to yourself; be trustworthy. You will never develop the essential quality of trust if you are a gossiper.

- DON'T be too cool. Cool people are never popular people; they are too cool!
- DO listen and be an encourager. Listening is a sweet fruit that is needed by all. It says that you care and that others are important.
- DO remember names. It shows others that they are important. The sweetest sound to someone is his or her own name.
- DO thank people.[1]

Be authentic. Be tempered by a godly character so the fruit of the Spirit is manifest and flows through you. Consider the fruits of the spirit (Galatians 5:22-25) and apply them to your life. Strive to live the way God intended.

The key aspect in helping improve your relationships will be the time you spend improving your spiritual life. This is what builds the Christ-like lifestyle we have been called to embody.

CAN YOU BE A GOOD PASTOR WITHOUT HAVING GOOD RELATIONSHIPS?

Questions for reflection, consideration, or discussion:

1. Why is it so difficult for some pastors to build good relationships?
2. In your opinion, what are the secrets to building good relationships?
3. List your five most important relationship do's and don'ts. Justify your answers.
4. What can you do to make yourself more available to church members?
5. Do you agree with The 50/50 Principle? Share your own concept.

Chapter 6

A STRONG FAMILY

A pastor's family is invaluable. Failure at home can lead to failure in ministry. If you cannot live happily with your wife and children, how can you counsel others and lead their families? You must devote the time and energy required to maintain a healthy home life.

A minister's home life is a greater influence than his pulpit. "Far more powerful than any sermon that can be preached is the influence of a true home upon human hearts and lives."[1] That is why Satan tempts us to neglect our home. He tries to keep the pastor so busy that he has no time for his family.

Many pastors seem to have the misconception that they must choose between work and family. The truth is, no pastor can be a good Christian unless he is a good father, a good husband, and a good citizen. A successful family life does not happen accidentally. It involves purposeful planning and work to develop the relationships within the family.

A TEAM MINISTRY

A pastor's wife is essential to her husband's ministry. But remember, she is the pastor's wife, not the church's wife. It is important to establish boundaries and not allow the stresses of work to suffocate your personal life. To do so, a pastor's spouse must share her husband's philosophy of ministry. It cannot be imposed. It must develop naturally. They must both recognize God's call to serve and dedicate themselves to the ministry. Ellen White says, "The Lord would have ministers and their spouses closely united in the work. The husband and wife can so blend in labor that the wife shall be the complement of the husband."[2] A pastor's family is not involved in his ministry simply because they happen to be his wife or children. They should understand that they also have a call from God to serve and as such, develop a philosophy of team ministry together.

FAMILY COMES FIRST

Communicating to your child the value of family is critical. There was a pastor who struggled mightily with family issues. He lived his life trusting that if you take care of God's business, God will take care of your business. He dedicated his life to the ministry, even sacrificing time with his family. He felt that because he was doing God's work, God would take care of his family.

I want to dispel this notion. We all have a responsibility to our families, as well as God. Without caring for our family, our ministry is meaningless. This pastor soon realized this truth and wrote, "If I am the greatest preacher in the world and lose my family, my ministry has failed. 'If a man will not provide for his own, he is worse than an infidel and has denied the faith.'"

> " *No success in public life can compensate for failure in the home.*"
> –BENJAMIN DISRAELI

1 Timothy 3:5 reminds us of the pastor's first responsibility—"If anyone does not know how to manage his own family, how can he take care of God's church?" We should strive for balance in our family lives as well as our ministry. Ellen White says, "Nothing can excuse the minister for neglecting the inner circle for the larger circle outside. The spiritual welfare of his family comes first. In the day of final reckoning, God will inquire what he did to win to Christ those whom he took the responsibility of bringing into the world. Great good done for others cannot cancel the debt that he owes to God to care for his own children."[3]

Jack Hyles, in his book *Let's Build an Evangelistic Church*, presents several reasons why no family should be more closely knit than the pastor's family.[4]

1. Because of the pastor himself. In many cases the loneliest person in the church is the pastor. Due to his responsibilities to all, he often has few intimate friends. Because of the fear of showing partiality, the pastor oftentimes leans away from any close personal ties. This should drive him to his family. Because of this situation, the pastor should solidify his family relationships.

2. Because of his wife. Oftentimes the pastor's wife is the loneliest woman in the church. Criticism and experience may have led her away from having close personal friends. For this reason she needs the blessedness of a happy, closely-knit home.

3. Because of the children. Whether we like it or not, our children live in a glass house. Whether we believe it or not, our children are considered different from other children. The pastor's child is often criticized. For this reason they must turn to their family. They must find fun, pleasure, warmth, and love at home.

4. Because of example. As spiritual leaders, we are an example for church members. We must lead the congregation to close home ties and a happy home life. The best way to do this is by example. We must live what we preach in our homes and personal lives.

TIME FOR RE-EVALUATION

I heard a story about a pastor's wife. Her husband died of a heart attack and she became a widow at the age of fifty. One of her friends came to her with a bouquet of flowers and attempted to console her. She spoke of what a fine man and pastor her husband had been. But the new widow stopped her and said, "I appreciate your good intentions. And I truly appreciate your friendship. But you really don't understand how I feel. I have never really confided in you about my marriage. The truth is, this last week has been the first week in 28 years that I have not been routinely belittled or criticized. It would happen at least ten times a day for a wide variety of faults, from the way I dress to the way I cook. This last week was the first time in a very long time that I awoke with peace in my heart and went to bed with joy in my soul. My husband was an accomplished man, a good provider, and a good leader. He was as good a father as he knew how. But he was not a loving husband and I really won't miss him as much as you may think I do."

One of the easiest things to do in ministry is to lose balance in your life. When you are serving the Lord, it is easy to neglect your family, yourself, and God, and to allow the ministry to take over your life. You must create boundaries to protect your life in the ministry. More often than not, burnout can be traced back to a failure to enforce boundaries.

Try to live well and build a good relationship with your wife and children. They are your church, your first ministry. Keep in mind that, "One well-ordered, well-disciplined family tells more in behalf of Christianity than all the sermons that can be preached."[5]

DO NOT NEGLECT YOUR FAMILY

Make appointments and regulate your activities. This will help you balance your responsibilities and make time to be a husband and father. Pay special attention to your kids and show them you love them. Plan family outings and focus on the needs of each of your children. They desperately need you. You must be there for them, helping as they mature, sharing in their tears and joys, and being a strong arm on which they can lean. Without that, your prayers and hopes for your family will be fall short. I often re-member reading about a pastor's daughter who said, "Every time I need to get help or advice from dad I have to make an appoint-ment with the church secretary."[6] How sad!

Remember, if you lose your family, you lose your ministry. Keep the fire in your marriage burning. Your wife has an extremely difficult role, both as mother and pastor's wife. She needs personal at-tention, loving affection, and time for her interests. Get away together. Make many special family days, which will build last-ing memories.[7]

> *A man travels the world over in search of what he needs, and returns home to find it."*
> –GEORGE MOORE

Many times we are so anxious for success in our work, we fail in its most important aspect—our own homes and families. This is our first responsibility. We cannot carelessly dismiss it for lack of time. If we are too busy to attend to our families, we probably should never have stood at the altar promising to cherish and love.

FAMILY'S CONCERNS

A survey conducted by *Leadership* magazine probed pastors' lifestyles, both at work and at home. Ninety-four percent of pastors feel pressured to have an ideal family. Twenty-four percent have received, or are receiving marital counseling. Sixty-nine percent of pastoral spouses work outside the home to make ends meet. The top problems in clergy marriages are insufficient time, use of money, income level, communication difficulties, and congregational expectations. Pastoral families share the same top stress factors of the married population in general—money, time, and intimacy. However, they also face the added challenge of constantly being scrutinized by others. This is why so many pastoral families are at risk of failure.

There is an increasing number of family problems among pastoral families. Divorce is on the rise and many children are leaving the church. This is not necessarily the fault of pastors and their spouses. Yet it does cause much suffering, and these families need our prayer and attention.

Congregations have various expectations of pastors and their families, whether expressed or not. They may vary from country to country, or culture to culture. Some are reasonable; others are not. For the sake of your family, you must identify and clarify expectations. Or else they will cause tremendous stress for you, your family, and your congregation.

STRONG FAMILIES

Family members must work to make the family strong. Like any relationship, people have to exert themselves to succeed. Each member has a role to play in strengthening the family.

A study of more than 3,000 families worldwide, over a period of ten years, identified six characteristics of strong, happy families.[8]

1. They are committed to each other. Those who long for cohesion within a family unit must place the family ahead of personal needs and desires. Their greatest desire must be a determination to stay together. Members of strong families are dedicated to promoting each other's welfare and happiness (Genesis 2:23-24). They value the unity of the family.

2. They have a strong sense of appreciation. A strong and happy family expresses appreciation for the big and little things. The words *thank you* are like music in the happy home.

3. They communicate well. Healthy relationships are built on communication. Without communication, there is no relationship. There are 10,080 minutes in a week. Out of all these minutes, the average couple spends less than 30 minutes a week in conversation. What does that say about our relationships? Strong families have good communication skills and spend time talking with one another (Ephesians 6:1-4).

4. They spend time together. Togetherness should be a priority for the pastor's family. There are many things that can be done together to increase a sense of family unity.

Eat meals together. A pastor's family should enjoy times of fellowship around the table. How sad it is when different members of the family eat at different times of the day.

Spend some evenings together. When you schedule an evening with the family, it is just as binding as a speaking appointment. Value your time with your family. Without it, it is impossible to grow together.

Travel to church together. I have made it a habit through the years to try to go to church together with my family. In other words, family members do not leave for church at different times. All of us prepare for church together, helping to dress the little ones and getting off to an early start to enjoy the trip to church. These can be precious moments.

Take a day off during the week. In many places, pastors are doing this. They recognize that family time is just as important as church appointments. This can be challenging when church members do not value the pastor's family time.

> " I don't care how poor a man is; if he has family, he's rich."
>
> –DAN WILCOX AND THAD MUMFORD

Vacation together. Plan a nice vacation for your family. Plan early. Remind the children about the number of days until vacation. One of the best ways to keep a happy family is to look forward to future events together.

Celebrate family worship time. Perhaps the one family in the church that finds it hardest to have family worship is the pastor's family. The schedule is interrupted so much and there are so many different activities that separate family members. If it is not possible in the morning, then take time to worship together in the evening.

Having boundaries between ministry and family life is often a tall order for clergy families, especially those who live in church housing. Yet quality family time is the one boundary that needs to be emphatically established and protected.

5. They are resilient. Problems drive weaker families apart while making stronger families come together. Strong families pitch in and help each other when times get tough. This is very different from families who place blame when tragedy strikes. Strong families see stress or crises as opportunities to grow (Ephesians 6:4; 1 Thessalonians 2:11).

6. They exude spiritual wellness. Healthy families involve God in their daily lives. They keep each other accountable for their actions. Strong families have a sense of a greater good and the power of God in their lives. This belief gives them strength and purpose (Acts 2:38-39; Deuteronomy 11:18-21).

Remember, a strong family is not immune to problems. They too face the same difficulties as other families—illness, unemployment, car accidents, disasters, death, and every other problem known to man. But strong families press on in spite of their challenges.

THE PASTOR'S WIFE

Pastors consistently report that spouses make a significant contribution to the health of their ministry. There are limited opportunities for pastors to develop close friendships with those outside of the congregation or with other pastors. As a result, the role of the spouse as friend and supporter is even more important. Here are some suggestions for improving and maintaining that relationship:

The pastor's wife is the number one priority, not the church. If you have been called by God to be a minister, it does not mean the church is your priority. You must make your wife and children your top priority. This means keeping their needs foremost in your plans and mind.

She should be involved in evangelism. Evangelism should be a part of her personal ministry. I have noticed some pastoral wives are rarely involved in aspect of ministry. They are not committed to missionary visits or Bible studies. They are tied up in the house with the children, and don't take an active role in ministry. As a result, they deny themselves the opportunity for spiritual growth.

She should make special visits with her husband. Church members appreciate having both the pastor and his wife visit their home. My wife, Raquel, often accompanies me on visitations. This has allowed for many pleasant ministerial experiences together.

She is not a church officer. Sometimes church members have stereotyped the ideal pastor's wife. They think she has to play the piano, perform special music, or at least be in the choir. The truth is, the majority of pastoral wives cannot play an instrument or sing well enough to be in the choir. The church should realize that her husband is the pastor and her best influence does not have to be in the church office. Everyone has a unique calling based on abilities, and the pastor's wife is no exception.

She is not the church hostess. She is not responsible for ensuring everyone enjoys the worship service. If things go wrong, or if someone is unhappy with her husband or with some aspect of the service, it is not her responsibility to fix the problem.

She is not the social organizer for the church. It is not her job to plan or even attend every potluck or baby shower. This is for church members to undertake as a body. The pastor's wife does not need to have everyone in the church over for dinner either. Hospitality is mandated for the whole church, not just for the pastor's family.

She is not automatically the Women's Ministries director. If she is not inclined to teaching, she should

> " *The family you come from isn't as important as the family you're going to have.* "
>
> –RING LARDNER

not feel pressured to teach Bible studies and Sabbath school classes, or be the Women's Ministries Director. No one in the local church should be elected by status, but by qualification and gifts. Of course, if she is gifted in developing a certain ministry in the church, then she can serve according to her spiritual gifts.[9]

IF YOU ARE NOT A PASTOR

If you are not a full-time minister, let me mention something here. No occupation is more difficult than ministry. With most jobs, at the end of the workday, one can go home and relax. A pastor cannot. A pastor and his family are scrutinized all the time. They are watched constantly.

Find ways to appreciate all that your pastor and his wife do for the church family. Take their children on an outing with yours. Wrap your pastor and his family in your love and appreciation. It is hard to rear a family while tending to a church. Make sure your pastor's family knows they are loved.

CAN YOU BE A GOOD PASTOR WITHOUT HAVING A STRONG PASTORAL FAMILY?

Questions for reflection, consideration, or discussion:

1. How do you practice the concept of team ministry?
2. In your opinion, why are many pastors' children falling by the wayside?
3. How do you spend your time with your family?
4. What are the three most important characteristics in building a strong family?
5. What are the most important activities your wife can do in the church?

A STRONG FAMILY

Chapter 7

AN EXCEPTIONAL VISITOR

Pastoral visitation has been critical to my ministry. It provides an opportunity to get to know and befriend my congregation. Every pastor has his strengths, weaknesses, gifts, and interests. Some emphasize preaching; others administration, or teaching. For me, visitation is the strength of my ministry. Some days, visiting is a joyful adventure; other days, it can be difficult. But my ministry cannot exist without it.

Pastoral visitation and its resulting friendships are essential to effective ministry. Ellen White wrote, "If he neglects this work, the visiting of the people in their homes, he is an unfaithful shepherd, and the rebuke of God is upon him. His work is not half done."[1] A pastor, who neglects visitation, cannot influence his people in a meaningful way.

Although this can be a challenge in pastoral ministry, it is important for shepherds to know their sheep. Jesus, our Master and ultimate example, said, "I am the Good Shepherd; I know my sheep and my sheep know me" (John 10:14). Pastoral visitation enables the pastor and members to identify with one another.

The Bible warns against neglecting this important ministry. "Woe to the shepherds of Israel who only take care of themselves! Should not shepherds take care of the flock? You have not strengthened the weak or healed the sick or bound up the injured. You have not brought back the strays or searched for the lost. So they were scattered because there was no shepherd. They were scattered over the whole earth, and no one searched or looked for them" (Ezekiel 34:2, 4-6). These unfaithful pastors of Israel failed to provide for the needy and chose not to seek the lost sheep. They focused only on their own needs. In response, God announced that He will hold the shepherds accountable for their stewardship of the flock. The same message applies to us, as spiritual leaders, today.

From my visits with pastors around the world, I've found that most pastors consider preaching their main concern, and give visitation little attention.

WHY ISN'T VISITATION A PRIORITY?

Unfortunately, pastoral visitation is no longer the norm. The old adage of the home visiting pastor producing a church going people might have once carried weight, but not anymore.

The decline in pastoral visitation cannot be attributed to a single problem. Some pastors may not have their own transportation. Security and budget concerns also present problems. In some countries, sheer congregational size can make visitation seem hopeless. Whatever the case, we cannot allow these things to compromise our dedication to visit our church members.

Undoubtedly, pastoral ministry is changing. With all the technological advantages at our disposal, we can end up spending the majority of our time there. Although it can be a tremendous help, we must avoid being seduced by technology to the point of losing personal contact with church members.

Many assume that after adequate sermon preparation, counsel, and general leadership, there is little time for visitation. In response, some churches hire visitation pastors to fill this need. Other churches establish visitation committees or teams to share the load. Visitation becomes a corporate effort. Even with a formal visitation plan, elders, deacons, and the laity should share this exciting ministry.

The pastor is not the only one in the church who can communicate God's love through a visit. He must actively foster this ministry if the church is to be motivated to participate in visitation. Encourage other members to participate in visitation as well. Visitation is a hallmark of a caring church.

Naturally, visitation will be easier for some people than others. Pastors with more outgoing personalities are more likely to make visitation a regular part of their ministry. Visiting is appealing to those with extroverted personalities. Their hearts go out to people who are hurting, lonely, or in need. However, this does not excuse those who do not have an outgoing personality.

To truly express concern and love for others, we must go where the people are. Laying aside our busy schedules and excuses, we must make people a priority. We must visit members in their time of need.

I once heard a gem of wisdom: *Excuses are tools of the incompetent used to build monuments to nothing. For those who specialize in them shall never be good at anything else.* Here are a few more reasons for a decline in pastoral visitation:

Perceived lack of time. Pastors are busy people, but the Bible teaches us there is a time for everything (Ecclesiastes 3:1-8). If there is a time for everything, certainly there is a time for visitation.

When it comes to your work, failing to plan is planning to fail. Treat pastoral visitation as an essential part of your ministerial plan. If you prioritize pastoral visitation, time will not be an issue.

The excuse of *not enough time* is a weak one. Pastors should better manage their time to make visitation possible. If you feel you do not have the time for visitation, you may need to re-evaluate your priorities. Weekly visitations must be planned. An intentional, regular visitation ministry should take precedence over administrative duties. Well-planned, organized, weekly visitation brings life and excitement to a church and keeps it from becoming self-serving and stagnant. Be flexible in developing the strategy for visitation that works in your community. Though not always easy, its reward is eternal.

> *Love will find a way. Indifference will find an excuse."*
> —ANONYMOUS

Complexity of life. A church member, explaining his absence of many weeks, said, "If you only knew how busy my life has been, you would understand why I haven't been attending. I work in the morning, I go to school in the afternoon, and I do my homework in the evening."

Most people find themselves running from one appointment to another, from work to home, from day—care to family commitments. When does anyone have time to sit and relax? Or for family dinner or exercise? Sometimes it's the members who don't have time for the pastor's visit. As a result of the complex life of church members, visits are now often based on need. Many pastors believe that the only reason to call on an individual or family is to sort out a need or to follow up on an illness or bereavement. No problem often means no visit.

I remember visiting a church family in a big city in Brazil. So happy to receive me, the husband commented, "Not once in ten years did a pastor or elder visit us. Because of this, I can honestly say we did not really know our pastor or elders, and neither did they know us or our spiritual needs." Some people may try to diminish the need for regular pastoral visitations. But I believe that pastoral visitation is an irreplaceable and critical component of pastoral ministry.

MISCONCEPTIONS REVEALED

Sometimes visitation is neglected because of negative experience, but usually it is because of misconceptions. There are two specific misconceptions that are particularly at fault.

> " The bad news is time flies. The good news is you're the pilot."
> –MICHAEL ALTSHULER

1. Visitation is an inefficient use of time. With so many under their leadership, pastors may feel that time spent with one individual is not as effective as time spent with the entire group. This is not necessarily true. The most effective method of ministry is personal time with an individual.

A good pastor will faithfully spend time visiting. "Pure religion and undefiled before God and the Father is this, to visit the fatherless and widows in their affliction, and to keep himself unspotted from the world" (James 1:27, KJV). A church leader who does not visit does not promote a pure religion. There are families, nursing homes, and hospitals where visits must be made. There are individuals confined to their homes who need regular visits. People with personal and family problems need to be visited. The needs are numerous; the laborers are few.

Again, visiting is not limited to the pastor, but he certainly should make time for it. His love for his congregation is expressed when he takes time to attend to them.

2. Visitation is too difficult to schedule. When you do not want to do something, you'll find a way to avoid it. Many pastors find excuses not to visit. These excuses include not expecting anyone to be at home, the weather being too hot or too cold, etc.

Everyone is busy. It may be difficult to schedule visits, but it is not impossible. Visitation enhances ministry and church health. The rewards of visitation well outweigh the challenges.

In my ministry, I schedule time for visitations. The morning is for my personal Bible study. Afterwards, I either have set appointments or just drop by. I've grown to learn my church family's schedules—work shifts, dinner times, bed times. Naturally, I try to work my visits around their schedules.

Visitation shows we are aware of our members' needs, that they are valuable, and that we care. Effectively done, it is a useful tool in assisting believers. Regular calls or announcements merely to induce people to attend more meetings or to enlist workers are inadequate as a spiritual objective. Visiting is caring.

Not all pastors, of course, will make visitation their top priority. Nonetheless, personal care for members remains a vital part of every pastor's ministry for at least three reasons. [2]

1. It is central to our call. To some degree, the words we use to describe our calling determine the nature of that calling. We call ourselves ministers, so we serve our people. We call ourselves preachers, so we proclaim God's Word. If we call ourselves pastors, that means we will also shepherd the church flock.

As we look at Jesus' ministry, we find the Good Shepherd visiting people where they lived. He stayed in the home of Mary, Martha, and Lazarus. He visited Peter's house and was also teaching in a home when a hole was made to let a paralyzed man down from the roof for healing. Pastors have an awesome opportunity to connect with families through home visitation.

2. People need pastoral contact. I think most pastors are very concerned about the spiritual condition of their members, but many think only in terms of the group and not the individual. Those who analyze our culture and business world emphasize the value of personal contact for leaders. John Naisbitt, in his book *Megatrends,* says that in a high-tech society people crave high touch. Effective management happens best through personal contact, the personal touch.[3]

> " *Tell me and I'll forget; show me and I may remember; involve me and I'll understand."*
>
> –CHINESE PROVERB

Visitation ministry demonstrates the personal interest that Jesus modeled. In our fast-paced, high-tech, impersonal society, people still need a human touch. Visitation expresses sincere interest in people and affirms their worth. To be effective pastors, we must draw closer to our congregation.

3. It is a ministry of love. Consider visitation ministry a process of extending God's love to people. As one minister puts it, "Pastoral visitation is incarnational: the Word became flesh and visited among us." You can be an extension of Christ for them, an expression, although imperfect, of God's love.

Do you know your sheep? When you are visiting your members, how many times have you heard, "This is the first pastoral visit I have had in 15 years?" Church members often feel unloved. If you are not convicted of pastoral visitation, then you are not fit to be a good minister. This is a ministry of love. "When the people see that you love them without pretense, then they will hear anything you tell them and they will bear anything you lay upon them."[4] By coming close to the human heart, you will know and understand its beat.

When you preach, you nurture people and demonstrate spiritual authority, but when you visit, you touch their hearts. Ellen White says, "When a minister has presented the gospel message from the pulpit, his work is only begun. There is a personal work for him to do. He should visit the people in their homes, talking with them in earnestness and humility. There are families who will never be reached unless the stewards of his grace enter their homes and point them to the higher way."[5]

God loves His sheep, both as individuals and as a whole. Through a visitation we bring God's care to His people. A deep relationship can be built between pastor and people, by making visitation ministry a long-term commitment.

VISITATION BUILDS BETTER MINISTRY

At one time in Seventh-day Adventist history, it was a given that pastors and local elders would visit members' homes on a regular basis. How else could they get to know their members and their spiritual needs? How else could they establish the familiarity and true fellowship that promotes honesty and accountability in pastoral relations? It was not just a mere suggestion. It was the duty of the minister to be consistently engaged in this process of visitation. Ellen White says, "It is not enough to preach to men; we must pray with them and for them; we must not hold ourselves coldly aloof from them, but come in sympathy close to the souls we wish to save, visit and converse with them. The minister who conducts the work outside the pulpit in a proper manner will accomplish tenfold more than he who confines his labor to the desk."[6]

How does pastoral visitation specifically enhance ministry?[7]

Preaching is enriched. Many pastors put in long hours studying the Word in preparation to preach. But in order to make preaching more relevant, it is vital to invest time getting to know the members. Pastoral visitation gives insight into the questions people have and the issues they face.

Often in pastoral visitation, we have to address the problems or challenges with which our members struggle. This could be a marriage crisis, unemployment, or their children's education. In many homes we have sick and dying members. Visitation is also a time to get better acquainted with their spiritual concerns. Any visit is an opportunity to get fresh ideas on how to help them and enrich our preaching.

> " *A man cannot be a good preacher unless he has a shepherd's heart.*"
> –CHARLES JEFFERSON

Shepherding people keeps your sermons original, vivid, and interesting. Shepherding helps you understand human nature—wants versus needs, vices versus virtues, books versus everyday experiences. How can you develop a sermon if you don't know where your people are spiritually?

Your sermons will be more powerful because you know your people and their spiritual needs. "But if the shepherd does not visit his flock, he knows not their condition, he knows not what truths to set before them, nor what is appropriate to their case."[8]

Relationships are strengthened. What do pastors gain from visiting members? Are pastors simply fulfilling their responsibilities? Or do pastors receive a professional and personal benefit from their visits? Pastoral visits cement relationships between pastors and their members. Since relationships are vital in Christian ministry, these visits help parishioners know their pastors. Confidence and the affection of members are also gained through pastoral visitations.

> *Shared joy is a double joy; shared sorrow is half a sorrow."*
> –SWEDISH PROVERB

Visitation is the seed for a relationship of trust. While the content of pastoral care should never show up in sermon illustrations, themes that emerge can be shared with many people.

Crises are prevented. By consistent visitation, I can often detect a crisis in the making. It might be that conflict, anger, or despair is just below the surface. Often, through an extended period of personal ministry, I can help a person get a grip on the problem.

I once visited a mother whose daughter was considering divorce. Later on, when I visited the daughter, she said, "I know there's nothing anyone can do, and it's frustrating. I feel so alone with this problem."

I responded, "But you have friends who can help you bear the burden, friends who can listen, understand, and pray with you about it." That visit was pivotal for both the mother and family. She had been discouraged with her daughter's marriage. I was happy to help. Aside from providing the suggestion that she talk with friends, the pastoral visit helped avert a crisis in the family. Pastoral visitation can also help prevent apostasy, dissidence, and heresies among church members.

Ministry is affirmed. Effective pastoral visitation gives the pastor a sense of accomplishment. Ministry involves many intangibles. Often success or failure is measured by an ill-timed comment mumbled by a disgruntled member on his way out of the Sabbath service. Most pastors could use a regular dose of satisfaction and affirmation. Visitation can provide this. It is here that we, as pastors, see the meaning of our ministry. We visit people in their homes, pray with them, smile and weep together, watch what God is doing in their lives, and help them grow in God's love.

To this extremely important work, pastors across the world devote many hours each week. We gently teach. We give assurance. We offer prayer. We keep families together. We comfort the grieving. We rejoice with the joyful. In so many words and especially with our presence, we communicate to an increasingly impersonal world of mass media that God cares for individuals, one by one, day in and day out.

Church attendance increases. In my experience over the last thirty years, church attendance in most countries is on the decline. Whatever the reason, pastoral ministry can make a change for the better.

It is amazing to see the results of pastoral visitation. People who are not coming to church are challenged to come back and recommit themselves. I have often observed that when families are visited, they show up at the very next church service, regardless of how long they've been missing. Church offerings also increase when pastors actively visit. It has been my experience that visited members are more financially supportive of the local church.

AN INVITATION

Reflect on the importance of visitation as you read the following quotation:

Ministers who sermonize without shepherding should be dismissed. There have been solemn duties neglected in accepting ministers to labor in word and doctrine who can only preach. They do not watch for souls as they that shall give an account. They sermonize; but the work is left undone which the sheep and lambs need to have done for them. And this half-hearted kind of work has been done all through America, and money paid to men employed, when they should have been dismissed to find work less responsible and care taking . . . . The flock of God have a right to expect to be visited by their pastor, to be instructed, advised, counseled, in their own homes. And if a man fails to do this part of the work, he cannot be a minister after God's order. The churches that have such labor are disorganized, weak, and sickly, and ready to die. The sermons are not vitalized by the Spirit of God, because the blessing of God will not rest upon any man who is neglecting the flock of God.[9]

If your relationship with church members centers on greeting people at the church door, you are losing out on the best part of your ministry. A connection solely at church is incomplete and does not strengthen your relationships. At the pulpit you can show your ability and spirituality to your listeners, but when you visit them, you touch their hearts.

IS IT POSSIBLE TO BE A GOOD PASTOR WITHOUT VISITING CHURCH MEMBERS?

Questions for reflection, consideration, or discussion:
1. What are the real challenges you face when visiting church members?
2. When it is not possible to visit particular families, what is your Plan B?
3. Does your church have an organized lay visitation program? If not, how could such a program improve the life of your church?
4. Besides the pastor, who in your church visits members?
5. Which areas of your ministry are enriched as the result of pastoral visitation?

Chapter 8

THE SIX ELEMENTS OF VISITATION

We should consider every pastoral visit a divine opportunity to communicate God's love through our time, presence, attention, and care. It is essential that, when we leave their homes, we have left more of God's character and promises rather than our own wisdom and thoughts in their minds and hearts.[1]

Many pastors seldom visit hospitals and go to homes only in case of emergencies. Their visitation is rarely regular or systematic. These days, many people have never had a pastoral visit. There is no excuse for this. Jesus went to homes as he saw need (Mark 1:29-31). He was a familiar guest in the home of Mary, Martha, and Lazarus. He regularly visited the home of Simon the Leper. When Christ commissioned his disciples, they were encouraged to go to homes (Luke 10:5). The pastoral care exercised by Timothy and Titus presupposed an intimate knowledge of the home life of church members (1 Timothy 3:4; 5:4-8, Titus 2:4-5).

Visitation has been ignored by so many because they find it arduous and time-consuming. Some even wish it would go away. But it will not, and they need to recognize its necessity in this impersonal age. Despite modern difficulties, there remains a longing in the hearts of church members to be visited and held accountable by their church leaders. Pastoral ministry must include visitation. It must be a part of our philosophy of ministry.[2]

GOD-GIVEN RESPONSIBILITY

God has given pastors the responsibility of shepherding His flock. Paul says in Acts 20:28, "Keep watch over yourselves and all the flock of which the Holy Spirit has made you overseers. Be shepherds of the church of God, which he bought with his own

79

blood." Peter echoes this in 1 Peter 5:1-3, "To the elders among you, I appeal as a fellow elder and a witness of Christ's sufferings who also will share in the glory to be revealed: Be shepherds of God's flock that is under your care, watching over them—not because you must, but because you are willing, as God wants you to be; not pursuing dishonest gain, but eager to serve; not lording it over those entrusted to you, but being examples to the flock."

This is no small task. Hebrews 13:17 says, "Have confidence in your leaders and submit to their authority, because they keep watch over you as those who must give an account." Pastoral visitation is a key tool in this oversight.

PREPARATION FOR VISITATION

Meaningful visits require preparation. First of all, use pastoral visits to take a spiritual inventory of your own life. Examine your relationship with God and with others. Determine your spiritual well being. Self-examination benefits you spiritually and helps fortify you against temptation and ensuing moral problems.

Secondly, take a few minutes to pray for yourself and for the family you are about to visit. Each day make it your goal to live a life of prayer. When you wake up, begin your day with prayer. Throughout your day, take a few moments to thank God for His help. Pray for the gift of love. Pray to be conformed to the likeness of Christ. Pray to be filled with the Holy Spirit. Pray to be a good listener. Pray for wisdom and insight. Pray for courage. Pray for grace. You should never leave without claiming His wisdom and spiritual protection.

Prayer is your most powerful tool. God wants to empower you with wisdom, discernment, patience, and self-control. Ask God for guidance and forgiveness. He knows your struggles and your limitations. He is always there for you. He will always listen. By speaking with God, you grow closer to Him.

PRIORITIES IN PASTORAL VISITATION

Even though they are stretched thin with responsibilities, pastors must be sure to make quality visits. In spite of possible frustration, visitations can be a rewarding experience in ministry. When planning a pastoral visitation program, it is important to set priorities. There are at least seven groups of people that require pastoral visits.

1. The sick. Visiting the sick is an important pastoral responsibility and privilege. In physically challenging moments, people are doubly blessed when we visit them.

2. Elderly. We should spend time making pastoral visits to aging members who are no longer able to attend worship, visiting them at home or in senior living facilities. These people can feel forgotten by the world. Forging a connection with their church community, even if they are unable to attend, can make a significant difference in their lives.

3. New converts. New members are in great need of direction and personal care. Frequent visits may be necessary to help disciple them. Time spent with them is never wasted.

4. Church visitors. When non-members visit your worship service, they need a visit in return—as soon as humanly possible. Go to their homes. If possible, take another church member. Express a few words of gratitude for their visit and invite them to return again.

5. Family visitation. Nothing helps us understand our congregation more than visits in their homes. It allows us to see, firsthand, the needs and pressures they face. We must be willing to go, whatever the cost. Visit them as often as appropriate and be careful not to show favoritism.

6. Missing members. This includes those who are not attending church regularly, no matter the reason. These visits show that we still care and can encourage them to return.

7. Local church leaders. As pastors, we depend on local leadership to help fulfill our ministry. Visiting with them helps build a common bond. It is the best time to deepen relationships and show our appreciation for what they are doing for the church.

I've heard many people say they've never had a pastoral visit. Pastoral visitation is time-consuming and tiring, but its rewards are evident. It can be seen through fellowship, the love members have for one another, and most of all in the progress of the Gospel of the Lord Jesus.

SOME TIPS FOR VISITING

1. Make a visitation plan. Plan to visit all the families in your church. Let the members of your congregation know you value pastoral visitation. Let them choose the day and time of the visit. Tell them that they do not need to prepare food or spend hours cleaning their homes. Emphasize you want to see them in their normal setting.

2. Visit by neighborhood. This will save you time and money. It will help make your day and week more productive.

3. Avoid going alone. Never visit someone of the opposite sex alone. Whenever possible, invite your wife or a local elder to go with you. Many pastors have faltered and lost their ministry by ignoring this precaution.

4. Have a backup plan. When visitation is impossible, phone calls can be very effective. They can be meaningful whether you address a pastoral concern or simply to wish someone a good day. A short conversation can lead to a word of prayer.

5. Keep visits short. It is always better for people to feel that your visit has been too short than too long. Try to keep visits around thirty minutes.

6. Share something. Whenever possible, give something. This may be a card, flower, balloon, picture, book, last week's bulletin, or any small token. A gift, however big or small, brightens the spirit and leaves a reminder of your visit. It shouldn't be costly. Leaving something with people is not a requirement for visitation, but simply a nice gesture. If you do not have anything to give, visit anyway. Your presence matters more than your gifts.

7. Break the ice. First of all, express interest in what is happening in your members' lives. As a pastor, your first concern is the spiritual welfare of your flock. But you should also show interest in other areas of their lives. I enjoy hearing about vacations, jobs, schools, and friends. Usually this kind of conversation helps break the ice and makes it easier to move onto spiritual issues. I agree with the old saying that people don't care how much you know, until they know how much you care.

Sometimes I find it helpful to share a little of my own life and family. I try to relate by showing them I have a normal family life with all of its joys, worries, and sorrows. Obviously, you have to be careful here. You do not want to spend too much time talking about yourself. However, some people find it easier to open up if the pastor himself is prepared to do so.

SIX BASIC ELEMENTS OF PASTORAL VISITATION

There is a great opportunity to accomplish several things when visiting church members. It is not my intention to present all the details of pastoral visitation, but to share its essential elements. There are at least six basic elements that should be present in each effective visit.

(1) BIBLE READING

A pastoral visit without reading from Scripture is incomplete. Taking your Bible on every visit declares that this book is central to your life and your ministry.

Select a few Bible verses appropriate to the special needs of the person you are visiting. Sometimes, you may not fully know the circumstances of those you are visiting until you speak with them. Elaborate on the scriptural passage to help apply it to the person's need. God's promises are reliable, and your visit can help them find strength in God's Word. When you use the Bible in pastoral visitation, you are saying that you value God's Word and believe in His power.

How the Bible Can Help in Visitation

The Bible helps us instruct church members in many areas of their lives. Here are more reasons to read the Bible during a pastoral visit:

It teaches God's will. God created us to live spiritual lives. But to live such lives, we must learn what He requires of us. As pastors, we want our members to embrace God's desire for their lives. Rather than giving them our advice, we should guide them to seek God's Word and direct them to the great biblical principles for everyday life.

As you share these biblical principles, your members may be surprised to find that God sets high standards for them, while providing a way to be holy and righteous through Jesus. Encourage them to learn how God gives strength in their weakness, and gives peace in their turmoil.

It gives God's direction. Reading Scripture during a visit shares God's plan with His people. As we study together, we realize anew the timelessness of the Bible. The Bible is just as relevant today as when it was written. Often when I experience trials in my life, I come across portions of the Bible that seem to have been written especially for me.

The Bible gives us direction in our lives by changing the way we think. As we read God's Word, our priorities change. We discover new directions that the Lord wants to take us.

It brings comfort in times of trouble. The Bible can be a great comfort. Many of us have gone through dark times in life, and found comfort in Psalm 23:4—"Even though I walk through the valley of the shadow of death, I will fear no evil, for you are with me; your rod and your staff, they comfort me." As we read these words, we sense God's presence in the midst of our despair.

Over the years, I have always found comfort in the Bible during times of sickness, turmoil, and confusion. God's Word soothes me. He has promised me peace, joy, and life abundant. Reading His Word affirms our need for His guidance. Never forget to take your Bible with you and read it on each visit so that both the members and you can receive a blessing.

(II) LISTENING

Being attentive and listening sincerely is an important aspect of ministry. A clever pastor can guess what people may say, but a wise and compassionate pastor gives them the opportunity to say it.

In general, people are better speakers than listeners. It is no different with pastors. What makes us poor listeners? First of all, we have never been taught how to listen. In school, we are taught how to speak, read, and write, but there are no courses devoted to listening. Dale Carnegie, in his book *How to Win Friends and Influence People,* says, "Be a good listener. Encourage others to talk about themselves." By listening, you will discover many interesting things about people. You cannot talk and listen at the same time. The ancient Greek philosopher, Diogenes, put it well when he said,

"We have two ears and only one tongue in order that we may hear more and speak less."

Pastors as listeners

Many people are in desperate need. But how do we know how to help without listening? What does genuine listening bring to relationships?

Respect. Listening shows respect for others. If I respect you, I will listen carefully to what you are saying. Listening shows that I am interested in what you have to say. It says that I am interested in you as a person.

Openness. Listening is a sign of openness to someone's point of view. When you are open to what people say, they do the same. Being open to other people's perspective makes them feel safe in their self-expression and more likely to be honest.

Presence. Listening means being fully present. You are not listening if your mind starts to wander. Listening requires patience. Listening does not necessarily mean silence. Be an active listener and show that you are engaged by occasionally asking for clarification or asking for something to be repeated. Being a good listener is an exercise in character building. The rewards are well worth the effort. The success of any relationship can be measured by the listening capabilities of both parties.

> ❝ *Put your ear down close to your soul and listen hard.*"
>
> –ANNE SEXTON

Pastors often focus on their speaking ability, believing that good speaking equals good communication. The ability to listen is an equally important component to successful communication.

(III) SINGING A HYMN

During visitations, a song should be sung. Although this may seem strange, it is not a new idea. As a small child, I used to sometimes visit church members with my father who was a local church elder. He used to sing hymns in members' homes. I have no idea where he learned this, but I could see how much people enjoyed it. Following his example, I have been doing the same.

85

I believe that hymns are valuable and powerful. When God wanted to impress His people with a message, He instructed Moses to write it in the form of a song (Deuteronomy 31:19). The book of Psalms is also a collection of songs used for praise and encouragement.[3]

The benefits of singing

Most of us are aware of the positive health benefits of good music. Apart from promoting a sense of joy, it can also lower stress levels. Regular singing can help solve many stress-related problems.

Jesus introduced the New Testament practice of singing in church meetings when He led His disciples in singing a hymn to the Father (Matthew 26:30). Paul subsequently exhorted believers to sing during church meetings (1 Corinthians 14:26). And they were filled with the Spirit (Ephesians 5:18-19). Many hymns contain sections of Scripture. Singing spiritual songs is an excellent way of letting the Word of Christ dwell within us (Colossians 3:16). Singing in church meetings or at home is an essential component of the mutual teaching, encouragement, and building up of the believers prescribed by Paul (1 Corinthians 14:26).[4]

It is also one of the most effective ways of teaching the gospel and inspiring members. A hymn is a prayer. And as such, it is a wonderful precursor to scripture reading and prayer.

Each pastoral visitation should be a mini-worship service at home, in which singing has a very definite place. As we sing, we bring joy and glorify God together. Family members should be encouraged to join.

Let us follow the Apostle Paul's teachings in Colossians 3:16 and never underestimate the importance of hymns—in teaching and giving thanks. Remember, God hears our hymns when we sing from our hearts.

(IV) PRAYER

A visit must include prayer. Prayer adds a special dimension. It demonstrates our dependence on God and allows His presence to change the atmosphere.

When we pray for others, there is a mutual blessing. God hears our prayers and understands that we want what is best for those for whom we pray. Praying for someone with an illness or for lonely people that need care in their lives can also put our own problems in perspective. Our prayers form a circle of blessing around us and around the people for whom we pray.

> **"** *Rich is the person who has a praying friend."*
> –JANICE HUGHES

Almost every day, I find myself in situations where I am asked to pray for someone. Praying for others is not always the easiest thing to do. Here are some basic steps that may aid your prayer ministry.

Know the person. Take a moment to get to know the person for whom you are praying. This accomplishes two very important things. First, it helps you know how to pray for the person. Second, it makes them feel more comfortable with you.

Don't assume. I have found simply asking the person what they would like to say to God very helpful. What would they like me to convey about them or their situation as I pray. Of course, they can pray for themselves, but they may not feel comfortable doing so. Asking them what they want to say to God makes the situation more personable and meaningful.

Touch the person. If appropriate, place your hand on the person while you pray for them. I don't believe this creates any kind of special connection or power exchange. However, I do believe this creates a more personal and intimate setting for prayer. A caring hand on a shoulder can go a long way in comforting the person for whom you are praying. But be careful of any touch that may be inappropriate, especially with someone of the opposite sex.

Pray from your heart. Pray passionately and from your own heart. Remember, you are talking to God and not the person to whom you are ministering.

Ellen White says "prayer should be a part of each family visit. Never enter a family without inviting them together, and bowing down and praying with them before you leave."[5] Prayer can be moving in any circumstance. But in the presence of others, it can create powerful bonds. The shared experience draws people together as they focus on spirituality. A genuine spiritual leader is always praying for his people.

(V) SPIRITUAL CHECKLIST

Doctors ask many questions to evaluate and identify health problems. Pastors are spiritual doctors and their task is much easier and more effective if they also ask questions to help identify spiritual needs. Ellen White suggests that pastors "inquire into the health of their souls. What does a skillful physician do? He inquires into the particulars of the case, then seeks to administer remedies. Just so the physician of the soul should inquire into the spiritual maladies with which the members of his flock are afflicted, then go to work to administer the proper remedies, and ask the Great Physician to come to his aid. Give them the help that they need. Such ministers will receive all that respect and honor which is due them as ministers of Christ. And in doing for others their own souls will be kept alive. They must be drawing strength from God in order to impart strength to those to whom they shall minister."[6]

The purpose of a pastoral visit is to have a conversation on spiritual matters. To avoid the impression that you are there to inspect or investigate their lives, have some crucial questions in mind to challenge them and encourage spiritual growth. Here are some examples:

> *Kindness is the language which the deaf can hear and the blind can see."*
>
> —MARK TWAIN

- How is your family?

- Do any of your family members want to be baptized?

- How do you find time for family worship?

- How is your personal communion with God?

- Are you able to share your faith with others?

- Do you have a Bible, Sabbath School lesson, *Adventist Review* magazine, and the Spirit of Prophecy books?

- Are you faithful in your tithes and offerings?

- Is church attendance a priority in your family?

- Do you have any suggestions to improve the church program or my ministry as a pastor?

- Do you have any prayer requests?

- Of what do your Bible studies consist?

- Are there any verses in the Bible or a particular doctrine that you would like explained?

- Are there any particular topics you would like to hear in an upcoming sermon?

- What gifts do you think the Lord has given you?

- Do you feel the church is making the most use of your gifts?

- What is your greatest fear for the future?

- Do you have any questions for me?

- Are there any areas in your Christian experience in which you are having problems?

- What do you especially like about our church?

- Can you point to areas in your life where you have recently grown spiritually?

The pastor must examine the spiritual state of those he visits. While it need not be protracted, everyone must understand that your visit is not a social visit.

In some cases, just one question can start a productive conversation. The ultimate aim is to discover how you can help them to grow and serve the church.

During the conversation, make mental notes of matters for prayer. In the concluding prayer gather up these various pieces of information and pray about each of them. In every visit, it is vital to show a profound concern for their spiritual state.

(VI) PROMOTE THE CHURCH PROGRAM
The best time to promote a church program is during a pastoral

visit and not on Sabbath morning. Many pastors promote missionary work on Sabbath mornings, encouraging members to "work" for the Lord. They say, "Let's work brothers and sisters! Jesus is coming soon!" When the church members hear this kind of promotion, they think, *Pastor, don't push too much. Today is the Sabbath; it is the Lord's Day, it is not a day to work. It is a day of rest.* They do not want to hear about work, even spiritual work, on the Sabbath. Every time they hear the word work, they are reminded of their weekly activities.

In my experience, visits are the ideal time to introduce, promote, and motivate church members to become involved in church programs. Present the program as a shared, communal activity. Stress that their support and participation is crucial to its success. Remind them that taking an active role in outreach provides an opportunity to express their faith. This experience fosters spiritual growth as we allow God to work through us.

When we share goals with church members, there is a stronger commitment to the mission of the church. We are able to better know the church members' skills and gifts and how to guide their application. With each visit our ministry grows. Sharing our passion for Christ will touch many. As pastors, we do not work alone. God gives us church families to work with us. Although we work hard, we do not always work wisely and try to do all the ministerial work on our own. This is why so many pastors are stressed, sick, and discouraged in ministry. Ellen White affirms the idea of shared workloads when she says, "God could have proclaimed His truth through sinless angels, but this is not His plan."[7] "Those who stand as leaders in the church of God are to realize that the Saviour's commission is given to all who believe in His name."[8]

In the final ten years I served as a church pastor, I did not lead even one big public evangelistic campaign. I spent most of my time visiting people in their homes and sharing the church programs with them. I challenged, equipped, and motivated them to be involved in church missions. The results were amazing. My church members were preparing people to be baptized and I was working with them.

Getting church members on fire for God and involved in missionary work is the best antidote against discontentment and stagnancy. "The spiritual life of the church can be kept alive only as the members make personal efforts to win souls to Christ."[9]

If you are a good evangelist and are baptizing 200 people each year, congratulations! But, if church members are not involved and working alongside you, the church is not fulfilling its mission. God's plan for the church is to preach the Gospel with the participation of each church member. Ellen White says, "If the church members do not individually take hold of this work, then they show that they have no living connection with God. Their names are registered as slothful servants."[10]

A CLEAR UNDERSTANDING

Job descriptions for pastors are rare. Over the years there has been resistance on different levels to establish a job description for pastors. Perhaps if a pastor knew that visitation is part of his job description, he would make it a regular part of his ministry.

The solemn word of the Lord, by His prophet Jeremiah, is applicable to the present time: "'Woe to the shepherds who are destroying and scattering the sheep of my pasture!' declares the LORD. Therefore this is what the LORD, the God of Israel, says to the shepherds who tend my people: 'Because you have scattered my flock and driven them away and have not bestowed care on them, I will bestow punishment on you for the evil you have done,' declares the LORD" (Jeremiah 23:1, 2).

Pastors always need to remember that they are privileged to be shepherds of God's flock. They are the flock of God the Father. They were purchased by the precious blood of God the Son. They are supervised by pastors appointed by God and filled with the Holy Spirit. They are precious and extremely valuable in God's sight. If the three persons of the eternal Godhead are so concerned for the well being of the flock, should not pastors also be concerned? If the Good Shepherd died for the sheep, should not we be willing to live for them? The Son of God shed His blood for them; should not others be willing to spend their lives in this service?

IS IT POSSIBLE TO CONDUCT A GOOD PASTORAL VISITATION WITHOUT THE SIX BASIC ELEMENTS?

Questions for reflection, consideration, or discussion:

1. What are your priorities for pastoral visitation?
2. Should pastoral visitation resemble a short worship service?
3. Why are the six basic elements in pastoral visitation important? Mention two benefits for each one.
4. What is your procedure when visiting a person of the opposite sex?
5. Mention other useful tips for pastoral visitation that are not listed in this chapter.

Chapter 9

A PASSION FOR MISSION

What is the mission of the church? Why are we here? Just as the church had a divine beginning, it has a divine mission. Seventh-day Adventists have a special message for these times—a unique purpose. Our church has an excellent mission statement and outstanding commitment to mission service. A good pastor reflects this passion for mission. He shares it with his congregation, and makes it a priority in church board meetings. He knows how to mobilize church members.

MISSION STATEMENT OF THE SEVENTH-DAY ADVENTIST CHURCH

Our Mission: The mission of the Seventh-day Adventist Church is to make disciples of all people, communicating the everlasting gospel in the context of the three angels' messages of Revelation 14:6-12, leading them to accept Jesus as personal Savior and unite with His remnant Church, discipling them to serve Him as Lord, and preparing them for His soon return.

Our Methodology: We pursue this mission under the guidance and through the empowerment of the Holy Spirit through:

1. *Preaching*—Accepting Christ's commission (Matthew 28:18-20), we proclaim to all the world, in these last days, the everlasting gospel of God's love, most fully revealed in His Son's life, ministry, atoning death, resurrection and high priestly ministry. Recognizing the Bible to be God's infallible revelation of His will, we present its full message, including the second advent of Christ and the continuing authority of His Ten Commandment law with its reminder of the Seventh-day Sabbath.

2. *Teaching*—Acknowledging that development of mind and character is essential to God's redemptive plan, we promote the growth of a mature understanding of and relationship to God, His Word and the created universe.

3. *Healing*—Affirming the biblical principles of the wellbeing of the whole person, we make the preservation of health and the healing of the sick a priority and through our ministry to the poor and oppressed, cooperate with the Creator in His compassionate work of restoration.

4. Discipling—Affirming the continued spiritual growth and development of all members, we nurture the newly converted, instruct them in righteous living, train them for effective witness and encourage their responsive obedience to God's will.[1]

OUR MISSION

We believe that God called the Seventh-day Adventist Church, not only to preach the gospel, but to call attention to oft-forgotten truths like Sabbath observance, Christ's Second Coming, Christ's ministry in the heavenly sanctuary, the state of the dead, health reform, and other truths we believe which are part of the three angels' messages (Revelation 14). Our message is not exclusive, it applies to all who disobey or ignore these truths. This is the great challenge before us.[2]

> *Sympathy is no substitute for action"*
>
> —DAVID LIVINGSTONE

The primary mission of our church is to advocate reconciliation between God and man. This is our supreme objective. People sometimes say, "What about the poor and the unfortunate? Doesn't the church have an obligation to them?" Yes. It is necessary to do good and relieve the afflicted, the needy and poor, but that is not the primary mission of the church. Preaching the gospel is the primary mission of the church because the church is God's agency to evangelize the world.

There may be varying opinions about the function of the church, but the following represents its four highest priorities:[2]

Proclaim the gospel to the world and make disciples of all nations. "Therefore go and make disciples of all nations, baptizing them in the name of the Father and of the Son and of the Holy Spirit, and teaching them to obey everything I have commanded you. And surely I am with you always, to the very end of the age" (Matthew 28:19-20). He said to them, "Go into all the world and preach the gospel to all creation" (Mark 16:15).

The combination of these two elements—evangelism and discipleship—are generally considered Christ's primary mission for His church. Evangelism is the ministry of proclaiming the good news of Jesus Christ that brings men's souls into fellowship with God. Discipleship is the training of believers to become disciplined followers of Jesus and His principles. It is the responsibility of every believer, not just pastors, to bring souls to Jesus Christ.

> " *If God calls you to be a missionary, don't stoop to be a king.*"
>
> –JORDAN GROOMS

Serve as a community of worship and fellowship. God originally made man for His own pleasure, to enjoy his fellowship and worship. Thus, part of the Lord's purpose for the church is to gather His people together and facilitate a corporate environment of worship, to express our love toward Him and one another. Jesus described these as the two highest ideals of Christianity. "Love the Lord your God with all your heart and with all your soul and with all your mind and with all your strength. The second is this: Love your neighbor as yourself. There is no commandment greater than these" (Mark 12:30-31).

The Lord is greatly pleased to receive the love and worship of His children, joined together in unity and love (Ephesians 4:1-4, 1 John 1:7). His presence is manifest in such an environment and authenticates our Christian witness in the eyes of the world. "By this everyone will know that you are my disciples, if you love one another" (John 13:35).

Build up believers and prepare them for missionary work. It is our duty to strengthen the body of believers and equip them for works of ministry. The church should be an atmosphere of spiritual edification, where God's Word is taught, where believers are grounded, discipled, and led toward spiritual maturity. This not only serves to anchor our faith in Christ, but also prepares us for service. According to God's plan, each member of the body of Christ is called to serve in some aspect of ministry (Romans 12:6; 1

Corinthians 12:14-31), especially as it pertains to bringing souls to Christ (2 Corinthians 5:17).

The church is the training ground from which we receive encouragement and support for our mission. It is a place where we learn how to communicate our faith to others.

Be a light to the world. Jesus used salt and light as metaphors for the influence of His church in the world (Matthew 5:13-14). Historically, salt has always been a valuable commodity used, among other things, as an antiseptic to combat infections. Light, of course, dispels darkness and is an essential element of life. Likewise, the church is Christ's righteous antiseptic to sin that displaces the infection of evil. The church is intended to represent His interests in the affairs of society. It was never intended to be passive or to be confined to a building. It is meant to be a beacon of God's high ideals to the world around us.

Christ wants His church to let His light shine in the world, while upholding the redemptive truths and righteousness of Jesus Christ. "Our people must learn to devote themselves to doing what is good, in order to provide for urgent needs and not live unproductive lives" (Titus 3:14). Jesus told His church, "Let your light shine before others, that they may see your good deeds and glorify your Father in heaven" (Matthew 5:16).

THE REASON FOR MISSION

Have you ever wondered why the Lord entrusted us with this crucial mission? Couldn't He have taken the gospel to the world through some other means? Ellen White affirms that "God could have proclaimed His truth through sinless angels, but this is not His plan."[3] The Spirit of Prophecy goes on to say, "God could have reached His object in saving sinners without our aid."[4] So what led Jesus to entrust His mission to human beings? In answer to this, White writes, "For us to develop a character like Christ's, we must share in His work."[5] There is a spiritual benefit in involving church members in missionary work. In the divine plan, those who sit idle fail to grow. Jesus came to this world to seek and save the lost. We were all lost before learning of the gospel. We were given an opportunity to accept Jesus as our Savior, and were saved. The great challenge of the Christian life is remaining within the experience of salvation. To remain in God's love and to grow in grace, we must study God's word and pray without ceasing.[6]

Most Christians discover that as time passes, they begin to lose their desire for

> " We talk of the Second Coming; half the world has never heard of the first."
> –OSWALD J. SMITH

prayer and Bible study. Why? "There is but one genuine cure for spiritual laziness, and that is work—working for souls who need your help . . . . This is the recipe that Christ has prescribed for the fainthearted, doubting, trembling soul. Let the sorrowful ones, who walk mournfully before the Lord, arise and help someone who needs help."[7]

According to Ellen White, the first purpose of missions is not simply to evangelize. It is an opportunity for men and women to grow in grace, to leave their spiritual indolence behind, and go forward strengthened. Inactive members, uninvolved in the church's underlying mission, are cause for concern. This isn't because outreach will suffer or baptismal goals may be unmet. It is because those members are missing out on a complete Christian experience.

Healthy Christians are committed to the church's mission. Sometimes we get confused. We think that the objective of mission is to baptize, so we invent new ways to baptize more people. This would be fine, if the purpose of mission was just to increase the number of members. But Christ intended mission to be an avenue for spiritual growth, as well. "There is no such thing as a truly converted person living a helpless, useless life."[8]

A MISSIONARY TEAM

When Jesus entrusted us with the mission of His church, He said, "You will be my witnesses." "And this gospel of the kingdom shall be preached in all the world for a witness." "You are the salt of the earth." "You are the light of the world." "Go and make disciples." All of these commands require individual participation. The Lord Jesus did not entrust His mission only to professional evangelists. We must make each member a missionary. Your challenge, as a church leader, is to keep watch so that each member fulfills his or her mission. "Let ministers [the church elder is a volunteer minister] teach church members that in order to grow in spirituality, they must carry the burden that the Lord has laid upon them—the burden of leading souls into the truth. Those who are not fulfilling their responsibility should be visited, prayed with, [and] labored for."[9]

> *The mark of a great church is not its seating capacity, but its sending capacity."*
> –MIKE STACHURA

"Wise is the pastor who learns early in his ministry that he cannot fulfill the entire ministry potential by winging it alone. The Lord chose twelve disciples. The early apostles selected seven quality men. The vineyard owner went to the marketplace to enlist help."[10] A pastor's responsibility is to train, organize, and lead the entire church in a concerted effort to warn and prepare the world to meet God.

No church member can rightly say, "I don't want to make disciples. I don't want to be a witness. I don't have the ability. I don't like that kind of thing, so I won't do it." The greatest reason for the church's existence is mission. It is not an individual or private matter.

In a survey of both ministers and lay members, ninety percent of pastors stated that the purpose of the church was to *reach the lost.* But ninety percent of the laity reported that the purpose of the church was to *meet their various needs.* Only ten percent of lay members stated that the purpose was *to reach the lost.*[11]

No wonder churches are not making a difference in their communities. They are not interested in reaching the lost and only interested in themselves. The church is constantly being tempted to accept this world as its home. There is no unity, no vision.

THE GREAT COMMISSION

When Jesus sent His disciples into the world (Matthew 28:10, 20), He sent them as a community, not as individuals. Even when the early Christians left their home churches to share the gospel, they usually chose to go in teams (Mark 6:7; Acts 15:22; 1 Thessalonians 3:1-2). Through visits, letters, and prayers, they maintained close fellowship with their home churches. The Christian community was important to their mission.

Christ has sent us into the world as ambassadors of His church. And as such, we share in its mission. Individuals working alone cannot accomplish many aspects of Christian mission. You can tell your neighbors about Christ without help from other believers. But it is unlikely that you will

> *The Great Commission is not an option to be considered; it is a command to be obeyed."*
> —HUDSON TAYLOR

be able to evangelize a continent, or feed famine victims, or build a hospital all by yourself. Yet, in partnership with other believers, you can do all of these things and more.

Our mission cannot be restricted to evangelism. The role of the church in this world is to lead people to God and to be reconciled with Him. Jesus taught, healed, helped, discipled, and served. The church must do as Jesus did.

MISSION AND PASSION

Passion is the combination of energy and conviction. True passion for mission develops from a love for God and commitment to His church. Ellen White comments, "It was the joy of Christ to save souls. Let this be your work and your joy."[12] She continues, "To save souls should be the life work of everyone who professes Christ."[13] Then she emphasizes this concept by saying, "Not upon the ordained minister only rests the responsibility of going forth to fulfill this commission. Everyone who has received Christ is called to work for the salvation of his fellow men."[14] Church activities such as prayer, thanks, music, fellowship, and other ministries are important, but taking salvation to the sinner is our greatest responsibility. This should be our greatest joy. In heaven we will no longer evangelize. But while we are here on earth, evangelism should be part of our life experience.

The task to proclaim the gospel to others is every Christian's mission—both yours and mine. The Great Commission has an expiration date, extending from the time that Jesus commanded it until "the end of the world" (Matthew 28:20). Each minute is precious. Even the demons know that time is short.

The Christian experience and spiritual growth requires witness. If we don't engage with our communities and share our faith, our Christianity is meaningless. What kind of church are we preparing for the Second Coming of Christ?

> " *The gospel is only good news if it gets there in time."*
> –Carl F. H. Henry

DIFFERENT MOTIVATIONS FOR MISSION

We are all motivated by different things—love, gratitude, fear, a desire to please. Each of these motivations is legitimate. Each complements the other. In God's universe, what is right is always smart. Sometimes we need all these incentives to do what pleases the Lord.

Though God's glory is the highest and ultimate reason for any course of action, Scripture sees no contradiction between God's eternal glory and our eternal good. On the contrary, glorifying God always results in our greatest eternal good. Likewise, pursuing our eternal good, as He commands us, will always glorify God.

REVIVAL, REFORMATION, AND MISSION

On October 11, 2010, the General Conference of the Seventh-day Adventist Church Executive Committee voted a document titled "An Urgent Appeal for Revival, Reformation, Discipleship and Evangelism." This document begins with a reminder of the mission of the Adventist Church to proclaim God's last day message of love and truth to the world. It goes on to admit that we are losing ground and, without change, we will not be able to complete this mission in our lifetime. The document concludes with a challenge to each leader and member to make the following commitments:

1. To personally place priority on seeking God for spiritual revival and the outpouring of the Holy Spirit in latter-rain power in our own lives, our families and our ministries.
2. To individually set aside significant amounts of time each day to fellowship with Christ through prayer and the study of God's Word.
3. To examine our own hearts and ask the Holy Spirit to convict us of anything that may keep us from revealing the charac-

ter of Jesus. We desire willing hearts so that nothing in our lives hinders the fullness of the Holy Spirit's power.

4. To encourage the ministries of the Church to spend time praying, studying God's Word, and seeking God's heart to understand His plans for His Church.

5. To encourage each of our church organizations to set aside time for administrators, pastors, health-care workers, publishing house workers, educators, students, and all employees to seek Jesus and the promised outpouring of the Holy Spirit together through a study of God's Word and prayer.

6. To use every available media outlet, conference, and workshop to appeal to church members to seek a deeper relationship with Jesus for the promised revival and reformation.

7. To urgently appeal to and invite our entire church membership to join us in opening our hearts to the life-changing power of the Holy Spirit, which will transform our lives, our families, our organizations and our communities.[15]

777 - Worldwide Holy Spirit Prayer Fellowship Initiative

Seventh-day Adventists are being called to pray seven days a week at 7 (a.m. or p.m.) for the outpouring of the Holy Spirit's power and presence. Praying any hour on the hour a person will join with thousands of others in another time zone around the world bringing unity. Ellen White says, "A chain of earnest praying believers should encircle the world . . . to pray for the Holy Spirit."[16] She also reminds us that, "A revival of true godliness among us is the greatest and most urgent of all our needs. To seek this should be our first work . . . But it is our work, by confession, humiliation, repentance, and earnest prayer, to fulfill the conditions upon which God has promised to grant us His blessing. A revival need be expected only in answer to prayer."[17]

Now is the crucial time in history and final events. It is a time, as never before, to pray to God for a deeper infilling of the Holy Spirit. It is time as pastors, church leaders, and members to be ready, to be sealed, to give ourselves wholly every day to Christ and to be totally dependent on Him. We need to receive the fullness of the latter rain, the holy oil, the sealing Spirit. This is our most urgent need. Let's seek God now to be revived, reformed, and empowered to accomplish the mission He entrusted us. Then we will be ready for Christ's second coming.

> *There are two days on my calendar— "Today" and "That Day."*
>
> –MARTIN LUTHER

THE REWARD

There may be innumerable crowns and types of crowns, and rewards unrelated to crowns. They are all graciously given by the Lord Jesus, and earned through the faithful efforts of the believer. Our rewards are given not merely for our recognition, but for Christ's eternal glory.

May we say like Paul, "The time has come for my departure. I have fought the good fight, I have finished the race, I have kept the faith. Now there is in store for me the crown of righteousness, which the Lord, the righteous Judge, will award to me on that day—and not only to me, but also to all who have longed for his appearing" (2 Timothy 4:6-8).

CAN YOU BE A GOOD PASTOR WITHOUT HAVING A PASSION FOR MISSION?

Questions for reflection, consideration, or discussion:

1. Why is it important for the church to have a mission statement?

2. As the "Remnant Church" what is our special mission to the world?

3. Do you agree with the four priorities of the church? Share your comments.

4. Why is church member participation in mission a challenge for many pastors?

5. What are the best strategies for mobilizing church members for mission?

CONCLUSION

*Rejoice and be glad, because great is your reward in heaven."*

–MATTHEW 5:12

You have been called to be a pastor. What a joy and privilege! Pastoral ministry is a *sacred work.* Providing His people with good pastors has always been one of God's central priorities (Jeremiah 3:15). I love being a pastor! Though it can be demanding at times, the rewards of being on the front line and seeing the gospel change peoples' lives more than compensate for the difficulties.

I am convinced that if you are called, the life of a pastor is the best there is. The rewards are numerous. I feel loved, appreciated, needed, trusted, and admired—all as a result of my occupation. I am an instrument God uses to promote the spiritual progress of His people. I owe a debt of gratitude to Him. I am honored to be a channel through which the grace of God, love of Christ, and the comfort of the Holy Spirit can flow to others.

The eternal reward of being a pastor far surpasses any frustration I will ever feel in ministry. I believe as John Calvin said, "It is my happiness that I have served Him who never fails to reward His servants to the full extent of His promise."

Our world is too busy and moves too fast. We are pushed *to do,* not *to be.* It is easy to work harder and harder, constantly pushing ourselves, and those around us, to achieve success. We forget that our drive to succeed can prevent us from taking the time to stop and listen to God's call. But wise pastors view their characteristics, skills, and attitudes through God's perspective, not their own.

I continually thank God for His kindness and support in my life as a pastor. I recognize that I have made a lot of mistakes. Yet, I hope I learn from them. I pray for forgiveness, wisdom, and discernment. I want to be a pastor after God's own heart. I want to carry out my ministerial work as a faithful servant. I know this is also God's desire. When I pray, my desire is for God to say *Jonas, don't give up. Keep growing, stand up and go forward.* Life and ministry are meant to be a great journey as long as I walk with God. Growing in my ministry is a process that never ends. Through this journey, we are not so much racing toward a finish line as we are striving toward becoming all that God wants us to be.

> **"** *Our reward in heaven will link us eternally to our earthly service for Christ."*
> –JONAS ARRAIS

This book does not end with a period, but a comma. The desire for continuing growth in ministry is a daily quest. No pastor can ever claim perfection. Pastors are on a journey toward Christ-likeness that will not end until we meet Jesus face to face. Then, finally, "we will all be changed" (1 Corinthians 15:51). Until then, pastors, keep growing, keep seeking, and keep up the good work!

I invite you to journey into the depths of your soul and to follow the Spirit's leading in the next chapters of your life.

Enjoy the adventure,

FOOTNOTES

CHAPTER 1 - THE ESSENCE OF A PASTOR

1. H. B. London Jr. and Neil B. Wiseman, *Pastors At Risk* (Colorado Springs: Chariot Victor, 1993), 183.

2. Paul and Libby Whethan, *Hard to Be Holy* (Adeliade: Oppenbook Publishers, 2000), 42.

3. H. B. London Jr. and Neil B. Wiseman, *Pastors At Greater Risk* (Ventura, California: Regal Books, 2003), 267.

4. Kevin Haag, *The Church is Full of Hypocrites,* accessed on February 10, 2011, http://www.new-testament-christian.com.

5. Robert R. Lutz and Bruce T. Taylor, *Surviving in Ministry* (New York, Mahwah: Paulist Press, 1990), 23.

6. Eric Liddell, *The Disciplines of the Christian Life* (London: SPCK Publishing, 2009), 29-30.

7. Dobby Mullins, "Integrity in Ministry," *The Mid-America Seminary Quarterly Magazine The Messenger,* summer 2007, 4.

8. Rick Warren, "How to Maintain Integrity in the Ministry," *Transparent Leadership,* January 2010, 17.

9. Ibid.

10. Ibid.

11. London Jr. and Wiseman, *Risk,* 182.

CHAPTER 2 - AN EFFECTIVE PREACHER

1. Richard J. Krejcir, "44 Church Growth Principles that are Real, that Work, and are Biblical!" accessed on January 5, 2011, http://www.starwire.com/partner/Article_Display_Page/0,,PTID34418_CHID771414_CIID1363062,00.html.

2. Steve Preston, "The Making of a Good Preacher" accessed on December 10, 2010, http://www.forthright.net/guest_writers/the_making_of_a_good_preacher.html.

FOOTNOTES

3. Jack Hyles, *Teaching on Preaching* (Hammond: Hyles, 1985), 89.

4. Ibid.

5. Ellen G. White, *Evangelism* (Hagerstown: Review and Herald, 1946), 185.

6. A. W. Tozer, "The Prayer of a Minor Prophet" accessed on November 7, 2010, http://www.sermonindex.net/modules/newbb/viewtopic.php?topic_id=34370& forum=45&1.

7. Wil Pounds, "Preacher's Preparations for Preaching" accessed on May 6, 2011, http://www.asermon.com/sermonworkshop/preacherpreparation.html.

8. White, *Evangelism*, 463.

9. Ibid., 280.

10. The Great Chicago Fire was a conflagration that burned from Sunday, October 8th, to early Tuesday, October 10, 1871, killing hundreds and destroying about four square miles in Chicago, Illinois. It was one of the largest U.S. disasters of the 19th century.

11. Ed Stetzer, "Contextual Preaching: The Key to Preaching So Your Audience Can Hear" accessed on September 12, 2010, http://www.edstetzer.com/2009/01/contextual-preaching.html.

12. Johnny Felker, "The Challenge to Excellence" accessed on January 10, 2011, http://www.truthchasers.com/Sermons/Expository/051902a.pdf.

CHAPTER 3 - A SPIRITUAL LEADER

1. Brent Filson, "The Arenas of Success" accessed on May 6, 2011, http://www.woopidoo.com/business_articles/leadership.htm.

2. John Piper, "The Marks of a Spiritual Leader" accessed on December 4, 2010, www.desiringgod.org.

3. William M. Mullis, "The Work of a Good Pastor" accessed on November 12, 2010, http://www.trumpetoftruth.org/Bible%20Studies/THE%20WORK%20OF%20A%20GOOD%20PASTOR.htm.

4. Ellen G. White, Pastoral Ministry (Hagerstown: Review and Herald, 1995), 96

5. Karen Hollowell, "Definition of Spiritual Leadership" accessed on October 6, 2010, http://www.ehow.com/about_5055232_definition-spiritual-leadership.html.

6. Piper, *Spiritual Leader*.

7. Ibid.

8. Ibid.

9. Ellen G. White, *Testimonies*, vol. 7 (Hagerstown: Reviewand Herald, 1902), 20.

10. Ibid., 19.

11. Clinton Shankel, "Field Test of an Instructional Program for Local Church Elders" (D. Min., dissertation, Andrews University, 1974), 5.

12. Piper, *Spiritual Leader.*

13. Ibid.

14. Pedusc Chidiebere, "A Good Leader" accessed on November 20, 2010, http://pt.tigweb.org/express/panorama/article.html?ContentID=9819.

CHAPTER 4 - A PRAYERFUL PASTOR

1. Jonathan L. Graf and Lani C. Hinkle, *My House Shall Be a House of Prayer* (Colorado Springs: NavPress, 2001), 36.

2. Ellen G. White, *Testimonies*, vol. 6 (Hagerstown: Review and Herald, 1901), 47.

3. Charles Spurgeon, *"The Preacher's Private Prayer"* in Lectures To My Students, (Grand Rapids: Ministry Resources Library, 1954), 43.

4. Charles Bridges, *The Christian Ministry with An Inquiry into the Causes of its Inefficiency* (Edinburgh: The Banner of Truth, 2001), 148.

5. Aiden Wilson Tozer, *Tragedy in the Church: The Missing Gifts* (St. Peabody: WingSpread, 1990), 62.

6. Richard J. Krejcir, "The Pastor's Prayer Church" accessed on July 20, 2010, http://www.churchleadergazette.com/clg/2009/03/the-praying-church-by-dr-richa.html.

CHAPTER 5 - A RELATIONSHIP-ORIENTED PASTOR

1. Richard J. Krejcir, "How to Build a Good Personality" accessed on September 6, 2010, http://www.churchleadership.org/apps/articles/default.asp?articleid=45956&columnid=4543&contentonly=true.

CHAPTER 6 - A STRONG FAMILY

1. Ellen G. White, *The Ministry of Healing* (Hagerstown: Review and Herald, 1905), 352.

2. Ellen G.White, *Pastoral Ministry*, 76.

3. Ellen G. White, *Gospel Workers* (Hagerstown: Review and Herald, 1915), 204.

4. Jack Hyles, *Let's Build an Evangelistic Church* (Hammond: Hyles, 1962), 65.

5. Ellen G. White, *The Adventist Home* (Hagerstown: Review and Herald,1952), 32.

6. Hal Webb, "Pastoral Failure" accessed on October 3, 2010, http://www.setlinc.com/webb/writings/pastoral_failure.pdf.

7. Ibid.

8. Nick Stinnet and John DeFrain, *Secrets of Strong Families* (New York: Little Brown, 1985), 123.

9. Nancy Wilson, "The Pastor's Wife" accessed on April 2, 2010, http://www.hissheep.org/books/the_role_of_a_pastors_wife_in_a_changing_urban_scenario.pdf.

CHAPTER 7 - AN EXCEPTIONAL VISITOR

1. White, *Evangelism*, 440.

2. Bruce Larson, Paul Anderson, and Doug Self, *Mastering Pastoral Care* (Portland: Multnomah Press, 1990), 17.

3. John Naisbitt, *Megatrends* (New York: Avon Books, 1991), 234.

4. Richard Baxter, *The Reformed Pastor* (Carlisle: Banner of Truth Trust, 1977), 32.

5. White, *Gospel Workers*, 187.

6. White, *Pastoral Ministry*, 225.

7. Self, *Care, 22-25*.

8. White, *Pastoral Ministry*, 192.

9. Ibid., 223.

CHAPTER 8 - THE SIX ELEMENTS OF VISITATION

1. Brian Croft, *Ministering God's Grace in Times of Illness* (Leiominister: DayOne, 2008), 90.

2. Irfon Hughes, "Visit – And Proper" accessed on May 6, 2011, http://www.banneroftruth.org/pages/articles/article_detail.php?735.

3. David Short and David Searle, *The Pastoral Visitation* (Scotland: Christian Focus, 2006), 10.

4. Kenneth W. Osbeck, *Inspiring Hymn Stories for Daily Devotions* (Grand Rapids: Kregel, 1990), 39.

5. White, *Pastoral Ministry*, 230.

6. Ibid.

7. Ellen G. White, *The Acts of the Apostles* (Hagerstown: Review and Herald, 1911), 330.

8. Ibid., 110.

9. Ellen G. White, "Work in Christ's Lines", *The Signs of the Times*, December 20 1899, paraghaph 6.

10. White, *Testimonies*, vol. 5 (Hagerstown: Review and Herald, 1882-1899), 462, 463.

CHAPTER 9 - A PASSION FOR MISSION

1. Accessed on January 9, 2011, http://www.adventist.org/statements/main-stat1.html.

2. Armando Juarez, "Mission of the Church," *Elder's Digest, April-June* 2006, 13.

3. Dale A. Robbins, *What People Ask About The Church* (Grass Valley: Victorious), 132.

4. Ellen G. White, *Christian Service* (Hagerstown: Review and Herald, 1925), 7.

5. Ibid., 8.

6. Ibid.

7. Marcos De Benedicto, Interview with Alejandro Bullon, *Ministry*, October 2008, 24, 25.

8. White, *Christian Service*, 107.

9. Ibid., 13.

10. White, *Gospel Workers,* 200.

11. W. Wilbert Welch, *The Man Your Church Should Know* (Grand Rapids: Kregel, 2004), 54.

12. Jim Fuller, "10 Reasons Why Pastors Leave the Ministry" accessed on May 6, 2011, http://pastoralcareinc.com/Articles/10Reasons.php.

13. White, *Christian Service*, 110.

14. Ibid., 10.

15. For more information concerning the Revival and Reformation initiative, visit: http://www.revivalandreformation.org.

16. White, "Our Need of the Holy Spirit", *Review and Herald*, January 3, 1907, paragraph 4.

17. White, *Prayer,* 116.